BEYOND
THE AMERICANS WITH
DISABILITIES ACT

NASPA
Student Affairs Administrators
in Higher Education

BEYOND
THE AMERICANS WITH
DISABILITIES ACT

Inclusive Policy and Practice
for Higher Education

Mary Lee Vance, Neal E. Lipsitz,
and Kaela Parks, Editors

NASPA
Student Affairs Administrators
in Higher Education

Student Affairs Administrators
in Higher Education

Beyond the Americans with Disabilities Act:
Inclusive Policy and Practice for Higher Education

Published by
NASPA–Student Affairs Administrators in Higher Education
111 K Street, NE
10th Floor
Washington, DC 20002
www.naspa.org

Additional copies may be purchased by contacting the NASPA publications department at 202-265-7500 or visiting http://bookstore.naspa.org.

Library of Congress Cataloging-in-Publication Data

Beyond the Americans with Disabilities Act : inclusive policy and practice for higher education / edited by Mary Lee Vance, Kaela Parks, and Neal Lipsitz. -- First Edition.
   pages cm
  ISBN 978-0-931654-90-9
  1. People with disabilities--Education (Higher)--United States. 2. College students with disabilities--United States. 3. College students with disabilities--Services for--United States I. Vance, Mary Lee, 1957- , editor of compilation. II. Parks, Kaela, editor of compilation. III. Lipsitz, Neal, editor compilation.
  LC4813.B48 2014
  378.0087--dc23

               2013050222

Printed and bound in the United States of America
FIRST EDITION

Contents

PART IV
Examples of Best Practices

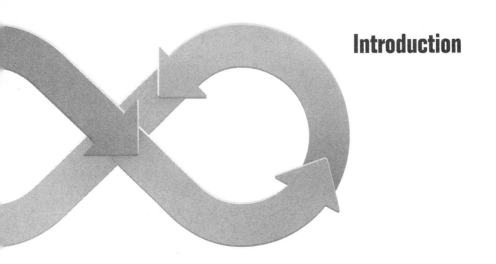

Introduction

Mary Lee Vance, Neal E. Lipsitz, and Kaela Parks

This book is for higher education professionals who work with students with disabilities, both apparent and hidden. It is intended as a primer and quick reference for administrators, faculty, and staff. It is not meant to address the accommodation process per se and does not prescribe adjustments or fixes for individual problems. Rather, it is based on the premise that accommodation alone cannot get us where we need to go and that individual adjustments are insufficient if our mission is to provide equitable learning experiences for all students.

As wounded warriors from Afghanistan and Iraq take advantage of their honorably earned access to higher education, it is even more incumbent on postsecondary professionals to provide a universally accessible learning environment. Colleges and universities should do everything in their power to remove barriers imposed by antiquated policies and procedures. Inherent in the roles of professionals in both disability services and student affairs is the need to work as agents of change, to spread the word that accommodation is just one part of the proactive, collaborative work. We have an ethical responsibility to build flexibility into the system, so that more people can achieve their goals for postsecondary education.

Disability services can no longer operate simply as an accommodation machine. Every chapter in this book emphasizes the need to move practices forward—to ensure that the accommodation process is clear and intuitive to navigate, while simultaneously working to minimize the need to have such a process at all.

The book is intended to provide transferable information that is applicable to any campus. It highlights the value of thinking inclusively (as in universal design pedagogy, with its commitment to total inclusion) and is intended to be future-focused, with information that will stay relevant for many years. It reinforces the need for student affairs professionals to maintain an ongoing collaborative partnership with disability services and the need for self-advocacy among students with disabilities.

Many student affairs professionals have little or no knowledge of disability services or of federal laws such as Section 504 of the 1973 Rehabilitation Act, the Americans with Disabilities Act of 1990 (ADA), or the ADA Amendments Act of 2008. For that reason, we sought contributors for this volume from both the National Association of Student Personnel Administrators and the Association on Higher Education and Disability.

The book is divided into four parts. Part I addresses the ADA and changing perspectives on disability. In Chapter 1, Paul Grossman focuses on the interpretation of the ADA as it relates to postsecondary education. In Chapter 2, Jean Ashmore and Devva Kasnitz discuss the development of academic models of disability and offer suggestions for implementing inclusive, person-affirming approaches. Chapter 3, by Sheryl Burgstahler, addresses universal design in higher education to accommodate the learning styles of all students by providing multiple teaching approaches, multiple methods to encourage student engagement, and multiple assessment strategies.

Part II covers information and communication technology. In Chapter 4, Rachel Luna provides an overview of the use and challenges of technology, including some guidelines and benchmarks for achieving accessibility and resources for accessible practice. In Chapter 5, Gaeir Dietrich discusses how to provide accessible technology on campus, focusing on the need for collaboration across the institution.

Part III addresses emerging and growing populations and their impact on higher education. In Chapter 6, John Mikelson describes today's veterans, as well as valuable resources and multiple ways to meet their needs. In Chapter 7, Tom Thompson articulates the need for higher education to provide postsecondary opportunities for students with intellectual disabilities and describes specific program models. In Chapter 8, Lorraine Wolf and Jane Thierfeld Brown discuss how we can foster success for students with hidden disabilities. They describe this heterogeneous population, areas in which these students may struggle, and strategies that can create a more supportive campus culture.

Part IV—the final section of the book—provides examples of best practices in student affairs and disability services. "Beyond the Minimum: Innovations and Partnerships" describes innovative funding models, as well as mutually beneficial partnerships that can be established through event planning. "Strengthening the Student Affairs Response Through Collaboration" addresses the benefit of cross-campus collaborations to meet the needs of students with disabilities. "Universal Design in Built and Online Environments" focuses on the need to ensure that infrastructure meets the needs of the students we serve. "Transition to College" highlights the differences between K–12 and postsecondary education, and the importance of self-advocacy, transition programs, and a multidisciplinary approach. "Experiential Education for Successful Employment Outcomes" describes NuConnect, a wraparound model based on a strategic partnership among career services, cooperative education, and disability services. "Accessible Recreational and Athletic Opportunities" suggests ways to provide opportunities for students with disabilities to participate in competitive and recreational athletics. "Accessible On-Campus Living" focuses on reasonable accommodations for students who need adjustments in student housing. "Study Abroad: Inclusive Opportunities" addresses barriers to access and solutions for accessible study abroad programs. "Engaging International Students with Disabilities" discusses how to remove common barriers and challenges these students face on U.S. campuses. "Student Conduct and Disability" outlines best practices for handling conduct violations by students with disabilities. "Intersectionality: Identity Re-formation" discusses how disabled students with disabilities can explore the many facets of their identities and harness the possibilities of intersectionality. Finally, "Challenging the Status Quo" suggests areas in which leaders in student affairs and disability services can advocate for the highest levels of access for their students and colleagues with disabilities.

Disability is a social construct. We constructed it, and we can deconstruct it. We cannot achieve a universally accessible environment without ADA compliance, but the ADA sets only minimal requirements. Adhering to them is like being satisfied with a barely passing grade in a class. We should want to be "A" students, and that means working toward a postsecondary educational environment that exemplifies universal access and full inclusion. Now that's an "A" concept!

PART I

The ADA and Changing Disability Pedagogy

Chapter 1

The Greatest Change in Disability Law in 20 Years

Paul D. Grossman

S tudent affairs professionals invest time and expertise advising and accommodating students with disabilities in part because it is the law, required of every American college and university that receives federal financial assistance by Section 504 of the Rehabilitation Act of 1973; of every public college and university by Title II of the Americans with Disabilities Act of 1990 (ADA); and of nearly every private college and university by Title III of the ADA, as well as by Department of Justice and Department of Education regulations and guidance that implement these laws. We also supportively advise such students because few, if any, discrete groups benefit more from higher education.[1]

These laws have recently undergone profound legislative and regulatory revision. To advise students wisely, professionally, and in a manner that respects their civil rights, we must update our understanding of the laws and their implementing regulations. Among the changes, the question of which students are covered by these laws is the most important.

Like food left too long in the refrigerator, a law can become "stale." Courts may interpret a law in ways that are seriously out of step with the original objectives of its legislative authors, and the law can produce unanticipated adverse consequences, exacerbating rather than solving a problem. In addition, unanticipated technological and cultural changes may place courts in the position of having to choose between guessing what a legislature would have required had it envisioned these changes or refusing to speculate in the hope that the legislature will recognize that the law needs amending.

Fifteen years after the passage of the ADA, it had become evident to disability advocates, employers, and educators that problems had developed with regard to interpretation and enforcement. A series of arcane and demanding interpretations of the ADA and Section 504 of the Rehabilitation Act by the U.S. Supreme Court had made it nearly impossible for plaintiffs to establish that impairments such as cancer, diabetes, epilepsy, monocular vision, bipolar disorder, or developmental delay qualified them as "individuals with disabilities" within the meaning and protections of the ADA or Section 504 (see *Sutton v. United Air Lines, Inc.,* 1999; *Toyota Motor Manufacturing, Kentucky, Inc. v. Williams,* 2002). Because status as

---

[1] Leading postsecondary disability scholars Burgstahler and Doe (2006) reported that "[f]or individuals with disabilities, a university education is highly correlated with career success. In fact, for people with disabilities there is a stronger positive correlation between level of education and rate of employment than there is for the general population. The employment rate is 16% for people with disabilities among those with less than a high school diploma, 30% for those who completed high school, 45% for those with some postsecondary education, and 50% for people with at least four years of college [internal citations omitted]." (p. 5)

4

an individual with a disability is a jurisdictional prerequisite to bringing nearly any claim under the ADA or Section 504, most claims of disability discrimination made in federal court were never heard on their merits. The laws had become ineffective in providing relief from discrimination on the basis of disability in both the employment and postsecondary settings.

The interpretations of the Supreme Court affected employment discrimination claims (including those made by academic employees) most, but students with disabilities were not spared. Students who alleged in federal court that their academic failings were due to the unlawful denial of "academic adjustments" and "auxiliary aids" (accommodations) or who challenged the denial of accommodations by standardized testing entities, such as the National Board of Medical Examiners, and state licensing agencies, such as bar examiners, usually had their cases dismissed on the predicate question of whether they were individuals with disabilities (*Gonzales v. National Bd. of Medical Examiners,* 2000; *Pazer v. New York State Bd. of Law Examiners,* 1994; *Price v. National Bd. of Medical Examiners,* 1997). Before the adoption of the ADA Amendments Act of 2008 (ADAAA), federal courts frequently reasoned that one could not be an individual with a disability on the basis of a learning disability if one had a record of academic success.

In addition to these judicial interpretations, many changes have occurred in higher education and in disability culture that the authors of Section 504 and the ADA could not have foreseen. Neither Congress nor disability advocates predicted that colleges and universities would be teaching a large population of individuals with acquired disabilities, such as the wounded warriors from Iraq and Afghanistan. Higher education is now presented to students who are deaf but do not understand American Sign Language and those who are blind but have no experience with braille.

Congress passed the ADAAA to address the definition of disability. The new law, which became effective on January 1, 2009, explicitly reversed the arcane and demanding decisions of the U.S. Supreme Court that made it difficult for a person to prove that he or she had a disability

5

within the meaning of the ADA and Section 504. Given the speed of technological and cultural change, it is unlikely that any federal agency will be able to stay ahead of the developmental curve. However, great advances were made in September 2010, when the U.S. Department of Justice (DOJ) published new regulations implementing Titles II and III of the ADA, applying to public and private colleges and universities (28 C.F.R. §§ 35 [Title II], 36 [Title III], 2010). These regulations concern everything from documentation of "disability" in light of its new definition, to defining a "service animal" and a "qualified interpreter," to setting comprehensive architectural disability-access standards for new construction and altered facilities. All the provisions of Parts 35 and 36 were effective as of March 15, 2012.

A New Definition of Disability

Student affairs professionals who are most affected by the changed definition of disability are: (1) career counselors and (2) advisors/staff in offices that provide services to students with disabilities. These professionals are supporting an increasing number of students whose impairments meet the less demanding interpretation of the term "disability," and they do not have to worry as much whether hard-working students and graduates will receive necessary accommodations on licensing and similar exams.

New Rules

The ADAAA and the Equal Employment Opportunity Commission (EEOC) regulations do not change the wording of the original ADA to define disability; the definition is still "a physical or mental impairment that substantially limits one or more major life activities [prong I]; a record or history of such an impairment [prong II]; or being regarded as having a disability [prong III]" (ADAAA § 12102(1); 29 C.F.R. § 1630.2(g)(1), 2011). However, through nine new rules of construction, the regulations implement the significant changes Congress made regarding how those terms should be interpreted by courts and entities subject to the ADA. As I often explain to my law students, the lyrics of the song are unchanged, but the tune to which they are sung is now quite different. After the EEOC issued its new interpretation of who is an individual with a disability within the context of employment discrimination, both the DOJ and the Department of Education's Office for Civil Rights (OCR) issued notices making it clear that the new EEOC rules also apply to defining when a student, parent, or any other person is an individual with a disability.

The following are the five most important of the nine rules of construction:

- *The term "substantially limits" requires a lower degree of functional limitation than the standard previously applied by the courts* (29 C.F.R. § 1630.2(j)(1)(iv), 2011; see ADAAA § 12102(4)). The number one ground on which courts based a determination that a person's impairment—such as a learning disability, psychological disorder, or mobility impairment—was not a disability was whether the impairment sufficiently limited a major life activity, such as learning, thinking, or walking. Now, an impairment no longer must "prevent or severely or significantly restrict" a major life activity to be considered substantially limiting (29 C.F.R. § 1630.2(j)(1)(i), 2011; see also 1630.2(i)(2)). However, a material degree of limitation still must be present—a routine allergy, mild migraine headache, common flu, or ordinary backache is unlikely to constitute a disability.

- With one exception (ordinary eyeglasses or contact lenses), *the determination of whether an impairment substantially limits a major life activity shall be made without regard to the ameliorative effects of mitigating measures,* such as medication or hearing aids (ADAAA § 12102(4)(E); 29 C.F.R. § 1630.2(j)(1)(vi) and (j)(5)(i)–(v), 2011). Thus, a student with attention deficit hyperactivity disorder (ADHD) or a psychological condition may no longer be excluded from the protections of the ADA or

Section 504 on the grounds that, with medication, the impairment does not substantially limit a major life activity.

- *An impairment that is episodic or in remission is a disability if it would substantially limit a major life activity when active* (ADAAA § 12102(4)(D); 29 C.F.R. § 1630.2(j)(1)(vii), 2011). Thus, the ADA and Section 504 cover a student with cyclical bipolar disorder or a person whose cancer is in remission.
- *The determination of disability should not require extensive analysis.* As a practical matter, this means that students who seek accommodations should not be subject to burdensome documentation requirements (29 C.F.R. § 1630.2(j)(1)(iii), 2011).
- *The effects of an impairment lasting or expected to last fewer than 6 months can be substantially limiting* (with regard to prongs I and II [persons alleging a current disability or a history of a disability]). Thus, for example, a student with broken bones, even if they will completely heal within 4 months, can no longer be excluded if the broken bones substantially limit a major life activity such as walking. However, a person with a "transitory and minor" impairment will not qualify for coverage under prong III (that he or she is considered or perceived to have a disability) (29 C.F.R. § 1630.2(j)(1)(ix), 2011).

Other Important Regulatory Changes

The ADAAA and the EEOC implementing regulations have brought about several other significant changes:

- *The list of examples of major life activities was greatly expanded to include reading, writing, concentrating, and thinking* (ADAAA § 12102(2)(A); 29 C.F.R. § 1630.2(i)(1)(i)). This increases the chances that a person with a psychological impairment, a learning disability, or ADHD will qualify as an individual with a disability.

- *A new type of major life activity pertaining to "the operation of major bodily functions" was added* (ADAAA § 12102(2)(B); 29 C.F.R. § 1630.2(i)(1)(ii), 2011). Examples are functions of the immune system; normal cell growth; and endocrine, hemic, lymphatic, and reproductive functions. Thus, a student with HIV no longer has to prove that the condition substantially interferes with his or her ability to procreate. It is sufficient that the infection substantially limits the functioning of his or her immune system.

- On the basis of these rules, *the EEOC has designated a class of impairments that will predictably meet the definition of a disability covered by the ADA (and Section 504)* (29 C.F.R. § 1630.2(j)(3), 2011). Examples include missing limbs, cancer, diabetes, epilepsy, bipolar disorder, major depressive disorder, obsessive-compulsive disorder, post-traumatic stress disorder (PTSD), and HIV infection (29 C.F.R. § 1630.2(j)(3)(iii), 2011). A doctor's note stating that a student has PTSD will be sufficient to establish Section 504 and ADA coverage. (However, it may not be sufficient to support the particular accommodations requested by the students.)

- *To achieve coverage under prong III, a person must simply show that an employer, school, or college regarded him or her as having an impairment* (see ADAAA § 12102(3); 29 C.F.R. §1630.2(k), 2011). Thus, if a student alleges that he was excluded from admission to a counseling degree program on the grounds that he had a psychological condition, proof that the admissions officer repeatedly referred to him as "crazy" may be enough to establish that he was regarded as disabled. This change to prong III is significant. First, many people who were unsuccessful in establishing prong III jurisdiction in the past, particularly for psychological conditions, will now be successful. Second, persons who can establish coverage under only prong III are not entitled to accommodations; however, they are fully protected from unequal treatment and purposeful discrimination, such as exclusion from admissions on the basis of disability or adverse treatment through a hostile environment on the basis of disability. Thus, a student who tells a counselor that she has been bullied by residence hall roommates on the basis of her perceived disability may have a viable claim if the institution does not respond through investigation and with appropriate interventions (OCR, 2000). Upon notice to the college, these duties would arise even though the student never registered with the disability services office, documented her disability, or requested any accommodations.

Students with Learning Disabilities

Students with learning disabilities will continue to face some challenges in establishing coverage, but they will be less burdensome than in the past. In the case of individuals who do not have an impairment that falls into one of the *per se* categories, a case-by-case analysis still will be necessary. In such instances, the EEOC regulations call for consideration of the "time, manner, and duration" necessary to perform the major life activity in comparison to "most people in the general population" (29 C.F.R. § 1630.2(j)(4) and 1630.2(j)(1)(ii), 2011). Learning disabilities such as dyslexia, are commonly diagnosed on the basis of intra-individual differences. Thus the question may be whether the intra-individual differences a student documents are of a materially greater magnitude than such differences for most people in the general population. Or, one might ask, in order for a student to read with the same degree of comprehension as most people in the general population, in what manner (how much more slowly) must that individual read? Exclusive reliance upon a bottom-line analysis, for example excluding from coverage a student with dyslexia because of a "high level of academic success," would not be consistent with consideration of time, manner, and duration as is specifically precluded by the new EEOC regulation (29 C.F.R. § 1630.2(j)(4)(iii), 2011).

10

Documentation

Despite the fact that it should be much easier for students to establish that they are individuals with disabilities, it is still important that they document the accommodations they seek. *Nothing has changed in the regulations that would require colleges or universities to fundamentally alter their programs of instruction, lower their essential academic standards, or provide accommodations that are not necessary to an equal education opportunity* (see 34 C.F.R. § 104.44, 2000; 28 C.F.R. § 35.130(b)(vii), 2010; *Southeastern Community College v. Davis*, 1979). The degree of documentation necessary to support an accommodation request should be determined on a case-by-case basis. Some accommodations will be self-evident and should require little or no documentation beyond what is observable or self-reported by the student.[2] A student in a wheelchair should not have to document the need for a schedule that recognizes the fact that it takes him longer to get dressed in the morning. However, a student with dyslexia who wants double or triple time on examinations might be required to provide documentation that logically establishes the need for so much extra time. For example, a college might ask for documentation that measures the degree of impairment in the student's reading fluency.

Test Accommodations

The new DOJ regulations concerning test accommodations, issued under Title III of the ADA, provide important guidance on accommodation documentation questions. These regulations are applicable to Title II entities as well (75 Fed. Reg. 56236, Sept. 15, 2010). The basic requirements provide the following:

- "Any request for documentation, if such documentation is required, [must be] reasonable and limited to the need for the modification, accommodation, or auxiliary aid or service requested" (28 C.F.R. § 36.309(b)(1)(iv), 2010).

---

[2] For expert guidance, well-aligned with ADAAA and DOJ regulations, see Association on Higher Education and Disability (2012).

- "When considering requests for modifications, accommodations, or auxiliary aids or services, the entity [must give] considerable weight to documentation of past modifications, accommodations, or auxiliary aids or services received in similar testing situations, as well as such modifications, accommodations, or related aids and services provided in response to an Individualized Education Program (IEP) provided under the Individuals with Disabilities Education Act of 1975 or a plan describing services provided pursuant to section 504 of the Rehabilitation Act of 1973, as amended (often referred as a Section 504 plan)" (28 C.F.R. § 36.309(b)(1)(v), 2010).

Service Animals

The term "service animal" is now limited to dogs (28 C.F.R. §§ 35.104, 35.136 [Title II]; 36.104 [Title III], 2010). However, the regulations also permit the use of trained miniature horses, in certain cases, as an accommodation (28 C.F.R. § 36.302(c)(9) [Title III], 2010). A service animal is a dog that has been individually trained to do work or perform tasks for the benefit of an individual with a disability. Any breed or size of dog may qualify. The regulation states that people with mental disabilities who use service animals that are trained to perform a specific task are protected by the ADA. Institutions that process service animal requests the same way they process other accommodation requests are likely to find themselves out of compliance with the new regulations. People who use service animals may be asked only two questions: (1) Is the dog required because of a disability, and (2) what work or task has the dog been trained to perform? Assuming appropriate answers, the level of inquiry or request for documentation should not proceed further.

For institutions with residence halls or sorority/fraternity housing, the Fair Housing Act and HUD (Housing and Urban Development) Section 504 rules (24 C.F.R. §§ 8, 9, 1994) apply. In addition to service animals, these rules require accommodation of people who, because of a disability, need an assistance or companion animal. An assistance animal may be of any species, and its function may include passive comforting actions. Here, standard accommodation procedures may be applied. Both service and assistance animals are available only to people with disabilities, are more than pets, must be housebroken and under the control of their guardians, and must not present a direct threat to the health and safety of others or create an undue burden that cannot be mitigated. The college may limit the use of the assistance animal to HUD housing. This would include the residence hall common areas, such as a dining hall, lobby, study hall, and TV room.[3]

Wheelchairs and Other Power-driven Mobility Devices

The regulations adopt a new two-tiered approach to mobility devices, one for wheelchairs and one for "other power-driven mobility devices (OPMDs)" such as Segways (28 C.F.R. §§ 35.137 [Title II], 36.331 [Title III], 2010). Wheelchairs and authorized OPMDs must be permitted in all areas open to pedestrian use. An OPMD must be permitted unless the college can demonstrate that the device cannot be operated in a manner in keeping with legitimate safety requirements.

Effective Communication

Interpreters are a required auxiliary aid for students with sensory impairments related to seeing, hearing and sometimes to speaking. Interpreters, remote or in the classroom, must be qualified both in terms

---

[3] An unsettled question is what to do if it is clear that the animal is not a service animal as defined by DOJ but the requestor is a person with a disability. Some commentators have suggested that, under Section 504, colleges may still need to consider, as an accommodation, making an exception to a no-pets policy for companion and assistance animals. The college might ask, does the presence of the animal reduce the impact of the disability? For example, a wounded warrior with PTSD might provide documentation from a treating psychiatrist that, in the company of the animal, the student is able to greatly reduce his or her necessary level of medication. If these commentators are correct, the use of assistance or companion animals would not be limited to HUD housing. If they presented no direct threat to health and safety, they would be permitted in the classroom setting and most other places on campus. It is hoped that further guidance on this question will be forthcoming from OCR.

of the student's communications needs and the nature of the content and setting. Both 28 C.F.R. § 35.104 (Title II) and 36.104 (Title III) (2010) now define a qualified interpreter as "an interpreter who, via a video remote interpreting (VRI) service or an on-site appearance, is able to interpret effectively, accurately, and impartially, both receptively and expressively, using any necessary specialized vocabulary. Qualified interpreters include, for example, sign language interpreters, oral transliterators, and cued-language transliterators."

Recognizing important advances in technology, the regulations concerning communication now include video remote interpreting (VRI) services as one kind of accommodation (auxiliary aid) that may be used to provide effective communication for students who are deaf or hard-of-hearing (28 C.F.R. §§ 35.160, 35.161 [Title II]; 36.303 [Title III], 2010). VRI uses videoconference technology over dedicated lines or wireless technology, offering a high-speed, wide-bandwidth video connection that delivers high-quality video images. To ensure that VRI is effective, the regulation sets performance standards. VRI may be an effective way to provide reliable and qualified interpreting services, particularly in geographic areas with a shortage of interpreters. However, OCR has cautioned that VRI as a substitute for onsite interpreting must be considered through an interactive process, on a person-by-person and even a class-by-class basis. Some students report that VRI is great for large lecture classes but works poorly in small seminar classes that require a high level of student participation.

The Internet has emerged as another critical communication setting. OCR has applied the principles of effective communication to both Web-based instructional materials and Web-based administrative services. In or out of the classroom, students with disabilities must be able to engage in the same interactions at the same time as their peers and with substantially equivalent ease of use (Resolution Agreement, 2013).

Equally important, in 2010, the DOJ began the process of establishing a regulatory standard for Internet accessibility. This objective remains on the DOJ legislative agenda and has been updated by separating Title II and Title III rulemaking, suggesting a goal of new regulations by the 25th anniversary of the ADA, July 25, 2015.

Ticketing

The regulation provides complex new standards for every aspect of the sale of tickets for accessible seating in both primary and secondary markets (28 C.F.R. §§ 35.138 [Title II]; 36.302(f) [Title III], 2010). Whoever is responsible for athletic and performance facilities needs to carefully study and implement these standards.

Accessible Design

The DOJ has issued revised ADA design standards that include the relevant chapters of the Access Board's 2004 standards (28 C.F.R. §§ 35.151 [Title II]; 36, Subpart D [Title III], 2010). Student affairs professionals should be advocates for an accessible campus, pointing out instances where students with disabilities face access barriers.

Identifying architectural barriers should be the responsibility of a well-qualified architect. The new standards attempt to minimize compliance burdens on entities subject to more than one legal standard by harmonizing them with the federal standards implementing the Architectural Barriers Act of 1968 and with the private sector model codes adopted by most states. As of March 15, 2012, compliance with the 2010 standards was required for any new construction, alterations, and barrier removal. The new regulations include a safe harbor provision under which elements in covered facilities that were built or altered in compliance with 1991 federal access standards are not required to be brought into compliance with the 2010 standards unless the elements undergo alteration. "Housing at a place of education" has been added at 28 C.F.R. § 35.151(f) (2010). The effect of this provision is to require dorms and similar student housing to meet the more rigorous standards of transient lodging rather than the less demanding standards that apply to residential facilities.

Additional Guidance from the Department of Education

In June 2010, the OCR and DOJ issued a *Dear Colleague* letter concerning the use of emerging technologies by educational institutions. The immediate concern was that colleges were establishing courses or course sections that relied exclusively on media technology (e.g., the Kindle DX) as the class textbook and that the technology was not useable by students with substantial visual impairments. For example, these devices lacked accessible text-to-speech technology. The two federal departments concluded that "use of an emerging technology in a classroom environment when the technology is inaccessible to an entire population of individuals with disabilities . . . [constitutes] discrimination [under the] ADA and Section 504 . . . unless those individuals are provided [with] accommodations or modifications that permit them to receive all the educational benefits provided by the technology in an equally effective and equally integrated manner" (OCR, 2010, para. 1). See also the Q&As concerning this guidance.

On January 25, 2013, the OCR issued a *Dear Colleague* letter concerning equal athletic opportunity for students with disabilities. The letter, which focuses on elementary and secondary schools, provides examples of how to achieve compliance with Section 504 and the ADA in existing competitive and extracurricular athletics programs. It noted:

> Students with disabilities who cannot participate in the school district's existing extracurricular athletics program—even with reasonable modifications or aids and services—should still have an equal opportunity to receive the benefits of extracurricular athletics. When the interests and abilities of some students with disabilities cannot be as fully and effectively met by the school district's existing extracurricular athletic program, the school district should create additional opportunities for those students with disabilities. (OCR, 2013, p. 11)

With regard to the postsecondary setting, the letter states, in part:

> The specific details of the illustrative examples offered in this guidance are focused on the elementary and secondary school context. Nonetheless, students with disabilities at the postsecondary level must also be provided an equal opportunity to participate in athletics, including intercollegiate, club, and intramural athletics. (OCR, 2013, p. 2)

As elementary and secondary schools create a critical mass of athletes with disabilities headed for college, and as wounded warriors interested in disability athletics return from Afghanistan and Iraq to our postsecondary institutions, colleges cannot afford to delay addressing equal athletic opportunities for students with disabilities.

Conclusion

The rules governing who is an individual with a disability and what forms of accommodation should be provided to these individuals have undergone some profound changes. More students are covered than in the past, but not everyone who claims disability status will be covered. More effective and reliable accommodations will have to be provided, although the rules do not require fundamental alterations in the nature of a program.

Disabled student service programs are well qualified to be the lead office in addressing these new requirements, but they cannot assume responsibility for campuswide compliance. Facilities offices will have to understand and implement the new architectural access requirements. Event managers will have to take responsibility for the new ticketing rules. Security staff will need to know the permissible scope of inquiries concerning service animals.

Student affairs professionals will play a critical role: They must understand the new rules in order to effectively counsel students with disabilities on the best ways to achieve their educational and career aspirations, on which barriers they no longer have to tolerate, and on where to obtain assistance in removing these barriers.

To facilitate success for students with disabilities, the campus must demonstrate that it values these students. Accommodations can be perceived as a burden placed on a college or university by federal law or as a source of innovation in teaching. Students with disabilities can be considered a group that is likely to lower academic standards or a group that is essential to campus diversity, enriching the classroom experience. The messages advisors convey in this area will have an impact not only on students with disabilities but on their nondisabled peers as well. In fact, advising degree programs themselves will need to attract students with disabilities so they can truly understand the benefits of having individuals with disabilities in higher education. Our colleges and universities need to do more to welcome these students and help them attain professional positions that both model and provide insight into overcoming barriers to academic and career success.

References

ADA Amendments Act of 2008, 42 U.S.C. § 12101 note (2011).

Americans with Disabilities Act of 1990, 42 U.S.C., § 12101 *et seq.* (2011).

Architectural Barriers Act of 1968, 42 U.S.C., § 4151 *et seq.* (2011).

Association on Higher Education and Disability. (2012, April). *Supporting accommodation requests: Guidance on documentation practices.* Retrieved from http://www.ahead.org/resources/documentation_guidance.

Burgstahler, S., & Doe, T. (2006). *Improving postsecondary outcomes for students with disabilities: Designing professional development for faculty.* Manoa, HI: University of Hawaii at Manoa Center on Disability Studies, National Center for the Study of Postsecondary Educational Supports.

Fair Housing Act of 1968, 42 U.S.C., § 3601 *et seq.* (2011).

Gonzales v. National Board of Medical Examiners, 225 F.3d 620, (6th Cir., 2000).

Individuals with Disabilities Education Act, 20 U.S.C., § 1400 *et seq.* (2012).

Pazer v. New York State Board of Law Examiners, 849 F.Supp. 284, (S.D. N.Y.,1994).

Price v. National Board of Medical Examiners, 966 F.Supp. 419, (S.D. W. Va., 1997).

Rehabilitation Act of 1973 §504, 29 U.S.C. § 794 *et seq.* (2012).

Resolution Agreement. (2013, February 28). *South Carolina technical college system OCR compliance review* No. 11-11-6002. Retrieved from http://www2.ed.gov/about/offices/list/ocr/docs/investigations/11116002-b.pdf

Southeastern Community College v. Davis, 442 U.S. 397 (1979).

Sutton v. United Air Lines, Inc., 527 U.S. 471 (1999).

Toyota Motor Manufacturing, Kentucky, Inc. v. Williams, 534 U.S. 184 (2002).

U.S. Department of Education Office for Civil Rights. (2000, July 25). *Dear colleague letter: Reminder of responsibilities under Section 504 of the Rehabilitation Act of 1973 and Title II of the Americans with Disabilities Act.* Retrieved from http://www2.ed.gov/about/offices/list/ocr/docs/disabharassltr.html

U.S. Department of Education Office for Civil Rights. (2010, June 29). *Joint dear colleague letter: Electronic book readers.* Retrieved from http://www2.ed.gov/about/offices/list/ocr/letters/colleague-20100629.html

U.S. Department of Education Office for Civil Rights. (2013, January 25). *Dear colleague letter: Students with disabilities in extracurricular athletics.* Retrieved from www2.ed.gov/about/offices/list/ocr/letters/colleague-201301-504.pdf

Additional Resources

For an in-depth study of college obligations under the ADA and Section 504, see the Department of Education's OCR Reading Room website at http://www.ada.gov/2010_regs.htm.

See also the DOJ website for ADA Titles II and III regulations, commentary, and guidance at http://www.ada.gov/2010_regs.htm.

The EEOC website for ADAAA and other Title I regulations is http://www.eeoc.gov/laws/regulations/index.cfm.

Chapter 2

Models of Disability in Higher Education

Jean Ashmore and Devva Kasnitz

O ur goal for this chapter is to introduce the connections between operational practices used in accommodation processes and administrative offices and the development of academic models of disability.
In particular, we contrast the pervasiveness of medical or individual service
models and practices (difficult to eliminate without conscious effort) with
the emergence of broader sociocultural disability models that underpin
the development and delivery of progressive disability services.

We explore concepts of disability, how disability fits into educational
environments, and the influences on disability offices across institutions.
The attitudes of institutional and disability office staff and the manner in
which services have evolved within the institution are critical to disabled

students' experiences. Burgstahler and Cory (2008) referred to both physical and programmatic design influencing disability practices:

> Our universities and colleges are often designed without regard to students with disabilities, creating a situation where such students continue to be marginalized through add-on programs, with negative outcomes as a result of issues related to attitude, expertise, legislation, documentation, and funding. (p. 576)

The academic discipline of disability studies has expanded concurrently with the growth of disability services as an administrative profession. In an ideal system, academics inform practice while practice supplies outcomes for research and development to consider. Unfortunately, that has not been the case with disability services. Progressive models of disability and the pursuit of universal access represent a direction—not an end goal but more of a process. We envision adaptable and sensitive models of how impairment is experienced as disability and how this lived experience can be part of a fair and positive experience of education and subsequent career and adult community life.

Disability affirmation and pride stemming from the disability rights movement and contributions from disability studies inform our choice of disability language, which may differ from that used in other chapters. We use the terms *disabled students*, *disabled people*, and *student who experiences disability*. This choice of terms reflects our belief that disability is a process.

Finally, although the chapter focuses mainly on students' experience of disability and campus disability offices, we note that disability departments have other consumers as well. Approximately half of disability offices surveyed by Kasnitz (2011) serve faculty, staff, and visitors.

History of Disability in the United States

Historically, disability has been a label for the experienced results of physical, psychological, or sensory characteristics perceived as markedly different from majority experience and thought to prevent people from participating in civil society. Disability was considered shameful to both the disabled person and his or her extended family, and was often regarded as a consequence of moral lapse. In *A Disability History of the United States*, Nielsen (2012) chronicled the many negative characteristics ascribed to disability over the years: "Inherent to the creation of the United States was the legal and ideological delineation of those who embodied ableness and thus full citizenship, as apart from those whose bodies and minds were considered deficient and defective" (p. 50).

Disability history has been shaped by the growth of medicine and the ancillary professions that diagnose, treat, and cure. Historically, access to education, transportation, employment, marriage, and family were negatively impacted by what the majority considered a pitiable condition. Institutionalization, forced sterilization, and restrictions on voting, work, and education are all part of the history of disability in the United States. Stigma and limited (or no) social standing and power were commonly associated with disability.

Disability-specific institutions (asylums) developed in the 1800s, most notably for the blind and the deaf. Pervasive practices that hid disability continued into the mid-1900s. Change began with the mobilization of parents and of armed services members returning from wars with injuries and disabling impairments. Veterans demanded employment and retraining. The civil rights movement, with its demands for equal education and opportunities, fueled the disability rights movement. In 1975, the Individuals with Disabilities Education Act ushered in a new era for disabled children, affirming their right to education. Section 504 of the Rehabilitation Act of 1973 affirmed the rights of people with disabilities to equal access and nondiscrimination in institutions, programs, and services that receive federal funds, including essentially all colleges and universities. The 1970s were pivotal, as the independent living movement spread across the country and demands for disability rights and access were loudly voiced. Disability advocacy was born, adopting the motto "Nothing about us without us" (Charlton, 1998).

The Americans with Disabilities Act of 1990 (ADA) and its 2008 amendments afforded greater access and protection from discrimination than ever before. With access to education and laws to protect from discrimination in all aspects of civic society, the disability rights movement came a long way in the second half of the 20th century.

However, laws and regulations still focus on people who are defined as disabled through an individual or medical model. Whether they are addressing education, employment, or access, these laws tend to be about individuals and what needs to be done for or to them. Even many hard-won improvements in the world of disability perpetuate the medical perspective that people with disabilities are defective and a benevolent society will do something specific to help them overcome their defects or (in a charity model) compensate them for their loss.

Simi Linton (1998), in *Claiming Disability*, summarized the effects of the medical model:

> The decision to assign medical meanings to *disability* has had many and varied consequences for disabled people. . . . [T]he medicalization of disability casts human variation as deviance from the norm, as pathological condition, as deficit, and, significantly, as an individual burden and personal tragedy. Society, in agreeing to assign medical meaning to *disability,* colludes to keep the issue within the purview of the medical establishment, to keep it a personal matter and "treat" the condition and the person with the condition rather than "treating" the social processes and policies that constrict disabled people's lives. (p. 11)

Many postsecondary disability offices use a medical model approach to service. Disabled students are greeted by an office whose title implies that students require support and burdensome processes that emphasize difference, thus creating a negative climate for many. Other student affairs units may opt out of addressing questions from disabled students, referring them back to the disability office as if it were a primary care entity.

Disability as a Contextual Variable

The World Health Organization (WHO) (2011) defined *disability* as a contextual variable, dynamic over time and in relation to circumstances but tied to a *health condition*. One is more or less disabled based on the interaction between the person and the individual, institutional, and social environments. Universal design (UD) is a way to reduce the experience of disability and enhance everyone's experience and performance (Story, Mueller, & Mace, 1998). The 2011 *World Report on Disability* noted:

> ... [disability] refers to the negative aspects of the interaction between individuals with a health condition (such as cerebral palsy, Down syndrome, depression) and personal and environmental factors (such as negative attitudes, inaccessible transportation and public buildings, and limited social supports). (WHO, 2011, p. 7)

WHO has purposely chosen neither to use a strict medical model definition of disability nor to limit UD to the built environment. In 2006, the civil rights of disabled people worldwide were affirmed in the United Nations Convention on the Rights of Persons with Disabilities (CRPD). The contextual component of disability is noted in the Preamble:

> [T]hat disability is an evolving concept and that disability results from the interaction between persons with impairments and attitudinal and environmental barriers that hinders their full and effective participation in society on an equal basis with others. (United Nations Enable, 2006, para. 5)

This convention, modeled on the ADA, has the potential to effect significant positive change for disabled people around the globe. International experiences of college students with and without disabilities could expand qualitatively and quantitatively during the 21st century as CRPD implementation enhances accessibility worldwide.

Social and Cultural Conceptions of Disability

Since the 1970s, disability advocates have raised critical questions that have resonated throughout the disability movement and contributed to the growth of the academic discipline of disability studies. Longmore (2003), in the introduction to *Why I Burned My Book*, wrote:

> Disability studies emerged in the 1980s as the academic counterpart to disability rights advocacy. It aims to do the work of research and critical analyses necessary to any effort at social reconstruction. (p. 2)

At the center of much of the work in disability studies is examination and extirpation of long-standing conceptions of disability.

> [D]isability rights advocates have argued that implementation of the medical model in health care, social services, education, private charity, and public policies has institutionalized prejudice and discrimination. Far from being beneficial, or even neutral, the medical model has been at the core of the problem. (Longmore, 2003, p. 218)

In his examination of the growth of disability studies, Linton (1998) noted, "[D]isability studies [have] demonstrated how the status and assigned roles of disabled people are not inevitable outcomes of impairments but the products of social and political processes" (p. 72).

The medical model of disability, historically pervasive worldwide both legally and socially, was called into question by alternative models that emerged from disability advocacy and studies. Longmore (2003) used the term "minority group model of disability" (p. 2). Olkin (1999) also explored the minority model, identifying similarities and differences between the lived experience of disability and that of other minority groups. Olkin noted that the nondisabled identify the inherent features of a person's disability as primary barriers for

26

the disabled, whereas people with disabilities cite as primary barriers those related to discrimination and negative cultural attitudes and practices (Olkin, 1999).

The term *social model of disability* was developed by scholars in the United Kingdom (Shakespeare & Watson, 2002). As Lee (2011) stated:

> The individual or the medical model focuses on the body as that which disables individuals. Whereas, according to the social model of disability, the disabling barriers are outside of the individual who has a single or multiple impairments. An impairment is the individual condition, while disability is socially constructed. . . . (para. 1)

Thomas (2004) examined the understanding of disability gleaned from disability studies and medical sociology, and expressed support for a social relational definition of disability:

> In this *social relational* definition, disability only comes into play when the restrictions of the activities experienced by people with impairment are socially imposed, that is, when they are wholly social in origin. (p. 581)

In the United States, professionals are likely to refer to social, socio-cultural, or cultural models, with the emphasis on the plural. All these theoretical models reframe the focus from individuals and their perceived impairments to beliefs, experiences, and societal practices that create and manipulate disability. Our preferred analytic descriptor—*cultural model of disability*—centers disability in the configurations and practices existing in and between societies that inherently disable. A cultural model of disability recognizes disabling barriers as not only physical but also attitudinal, procedural, legal, religious, historical, and linguistic. We posit that these social constructions of disability are inextricably and subconsciously woven into dominant culture, including postsecondary education; thus, the use of *cultural model* as a comprehensive term.

Evidence of ingrained cultural assumptions about disability can be seen in many disability offices on college campuses. "Support" is often part of the department's name: Disability Support Services, which has a medical overtone and is an example of "ableism." This use carries with it societal sanctions and beliefs that disabled students require support because of whatever disables them (Cherney, 2011).

Each model has economic impacts. In the medical model, the disability requires a special type of equipment or adaptation to equipment, which is often quite costly. Throughout history, access to adaptive equipment was usually available only to those who could afford it. In *FDR's Splendid Deception* (Gallagher, 1985), a history of Franklin Delano Roosevelt's experiences with polio, it is often mentioned that disabled people who did not have his resources had limited access to treatments, therapies, and adaptive equipment. The negative economics of disability (positive from the perspective of vendors) is apparent in the design of equipment, which often requires expensive add-ons so it can be used by people who access it in ways that were not considered in the product's design. When universal access features are incorporated into equipment, especially technology, costs for disabled and nondisabled users are equalized.

Medical and cultural models of disability significantly affect the experiences of students in postsecondary education. The medical model locates problems in the individual, whereas sociocultural models locate problems in the sociopolitical and institutional components of society. How disability is conceptualized—medically or culturally—influences structure and practices in colleges and universities. In evaluating whether the cultural model of disability is at work in disability offices and the greater institutional community, we can look at these areas:

- **Textbooks.** Is the availability of alternative formats considered in adopting instructional materials?
- **Instruction.** Are concepts of universally designed instruction used in course development?

- **Accommodations.** Is an individualized process applied to courses (i.e., what each course requires of students) when determining whether accommodations for students are necessary?
- **Access.** Does an architect or building designer use UD concepts to achieve usable spaces that maximize equality of experience?

Postsecondary Education and Progressive Models of Disability

Postsecondary disability practices grew out of antidiscrimination legislation and practices in special education. Most disability offices have traditionally focused on an individual accommodation approach. The emergence of the social and cultural models of disability—with the belief that human variation is a natural part of the diversity of life rather than a deficit—has challenged the disability office and the entire academic community to examine their practices.

The expansion of the concepts of UD into education has been instrumental in the evolution of disability services as well as instruction in higher education. When a disability office adopts a UD philosophy—that access for all leads to equality of opportunity and experience and a reduced need for individual accommodations—its role and engagement with campus constituents changes. Marginalization and separate treatment are reduced or even eliminated when the experience of students or faculty members with and without disability is equivalent. Universally designed campuses and curricula, while not utopian, can result in more meaningful and full access for all. The following are examples of a college student's experience at an institution that embraces universal access:

- **Offices offer varied means for interaction.** For example, different seating and counter heights; written and audio recorded information; distance and in-person methods; and forms that are accessible for people who will access them through varied means.

- **Individual difference is recognized universally.** For example, food contents posted in cafeterias enable people to meet their individual dietary needs with ease; financial aid procedures encourage all students to confidentially identify any circumstances that affect their financial status; and all classrooms offer various seating options.
- **Access is built in rather than by request.** For example, sign language interpreters are at all major campus events, such as graduations, and tickets to accessible seating at events are obtained in the same manner as those to other seats.

Disability departments are gradually expanding their reach within institutions, reflecting changes in philosophy and practice. At the core of these changes are the beliefs that the person who experiences disability is the best person to understand his or her circumstances and that the disability professional is an advocate for universal access to reduce or eliminate barriers. Any remaining individual accommodations should be approached collaboratively and creatively.

Guzman and Balcazar (2010), in a study of providers' perceptions of disability, identified three approaches to service provision: the individual approach, the social approach, and the universal approach. These three approaches are similar to the models presented in this chapter and reflect a broadening of perspectives, beliefs, and institutional engagement in disability services. Cory, White, and Stuckey (2010) discussed going beyond compliance and the positive outcomes of collaborative efforts of students and disability services allies to create inclusive environments at Syracuse University. The best approach is a quickly adapting hybrid. A cultural approach could be another way to define disability and campuswide service provision. Culture includes individuals, social groups, and environments and is all-encompassing. Culture change redefines progress and operational practices. Changes in the culture of disability are essential for inclusive and flexible assessment of school success and individual contributions.

Higher education should be a career path for disabled students, not just a directionless way to fill years.

In 2012, the Association on Higher Education and Disability adopted guidance for disability professionals about documentation in making determinations about reasonable accommodations. This guidance values the experience of the disabled student and encourages staff to incorporate student self-reports when they are making accommodation determinations, rather than expecting the student to provide extensive medical proof of disability and the need for accommodations. This approach tempers the strict medical model. Personal experiences of disability, social impacts of impairment that disable, and barriers in the academic environment all become central elements in accommodation determinations. The disability professional's knowledge of course requirements, campus features, and all aspects of the institutional experience are essential to effective collaboration with the disabled student.

Referring back to our lens-of-disability experience, campus disability departments should be catalysts that inspire educational communities to identify their dominant culture of disability, as well as the barriers in the environment (especially those that result in disabled students having experiences unlike those of nondisabled students) and how disability is addressed or incorporated into the curriculum (Linton, 1998). Examining these aspects of disability in higher education is essential to move beyond medical models of practice.

Conclusion

The precepts underlying universal access, along with social and cultural conceptions of disability, can lead to new disability cultures and more disability-inclusive practices on college and university campuses. The medical model under which disability offices developed and continue to practice can be supplanted by a richer, more inclusive set of practices that embrace cultural and social models. This movement is reflected in department titles that are moving away from "support" and even "service" to "resources" and by the updated standards for disability resources and services adopted in 2013 by the Council for the Advancement of Standards in Higher Education. Traditional-age students with disabilities can be described as the ADA Generation—they are generally well-versed in disability rights and have a sense of pride, which puts them ahead of out-of-sync college staff. Gary Wunder (2013), editor of *Braille Monitor*, called for equal access and equivalent opportunity: "We insist on the same book at the same price and at the same time it is available to others" (para. 23).

Disability offices, often rooted in outmoded 20th century practices and beliefs, will need to catch up to this new generation. As Amanda Kraus (2010) noted:

> Perhaps the role of service provider should not be limited to determining individual accommodations and facilitating campus access, but expanded to that of an ambassador of disability culture. We have the unique opportunity to reframe disability, push forward progressive ways of thinking, and challenge antiquated ideas. In our roles, we represent disability to our campuses and community. (p. 28)

Intention underlies design, and this applies to all areas of a higher education institution. Specific to disability offices, Thornton and Downs (2010) wrote:

> As disability resource professionals frame their role as the designers of the service environment, the focus shifts toward creating a usable, equitable environment in the disability office and beyond. In doing so, the disability office becomes a model of universal design and the social response to disability. This role offers great potential for facilitating and sustaining change on the campus at large. (p. 79)

Institutional practices, especially those related to disability, are influenced by history. As change agents, disability professionals and the entire institutional community must move beyond medical models and commit to adapting our policies and practices to align with broad-ranging cultural and social models of disability.

References

ADA Amendments Act of 2008, 42 U.S.C. § 12101 note (2011).

Americans with Disabilities Act of 1990, 42 U.S.C., § 12101 *et seq.* (2011).

Association on Higher Education and Disability. (2012, April). *Supporting accommodation requests: Guidance on documentation practices.* Retrieved from http://www.ahead.org/resources/documentation-guidance

Burgstahler, S., & Cory, R. (2008). Moving in from the margins: From accommodation to Universal Design. In. S. Gobel & S. Danforth (Eds.), *Disability and the politics of education: An international reader* (pp. 561–581). New York, NY: Peter Lang Publishing.

Charlton, J. (1998). *Nothing about us without us: Disability oppression and empowerment.* Berkeley, CA: University of California Press.

Cherney, J. (2011). The rhetoric of ableism. *Disability Studies Quarterly, 31*(3). Retrieved from http://dsq-sds.org/article/view/1665/1606

Cory, R., White, J., & Stuckey, Z. (2010). Using disability studies theory to change disability services: A case study in student activism. *Journal of Postsecondary Education and Disability, 23*(1), 29–37.

Council for the Advancement of Standards in Higher Education. (2013, May). *Disability resources and services.* Washington, DC: Author.

Gallagher, H. (1985). *FDR's splendid deception.* New York, NY: Dodd, Mead & Company.

Guzman, A., & Balcazar, F. (2010). Disability services' standards and the worldviews guiding their implementation. *Journal of Postsecondary Education and Disability, 23*(1), 50–61.

Individuals with Disabilities Education Act, 20 U.S.C., § 1400 *et seq.* (2012).

Kasnitz, D. (2011). *The 2010 biennial AHEAD survey of disability services and resource professionals in higher education.* Retrieved from http://www.ahead.org

Kraus, A. (2010). Professional perspective. *Journal of Postsecondary Education and Disability, 23*(1), 28.

Lee, S. (2011). Disability studies and the language of physical education curriculum. *Disability Studies Quarterly, 31*(2). Retrieved from http://dsq-sds.org/article/view/1587/1555

Linton, S. (1998). *Claiming disability: Knowledge and identity.* New York, NY: New York University Press.

Longmore, P. (2003). *Why I burned my book and other essays on disability.* Philadelphia, PA: Temple University Press.

Nielsen, K. (2012). *A disability history of the United States.* Boston, MA: Beacon Press.

Olkin, R. (1999). *What psychotherapists should know about disability.* New York, NY: The Guilford Press.

Rehabilitation Act of 1973 §504, 29 U.S.C. § 794 (2012).

Shakespeare, T., & Watson, N. (2002). The social model of disability—An outdated ideology? *Research in Social Science and Disability, 2,* 9–28.

Story, M., Mueller, J., & Mace, R. (1998). *The universal design file: Designing for people of all ages and abilities.* North Carolina State University, Center for Universal Design. Retrieved from http://www.ncsu.edu/ncsu/design/cud/pubs_p/pudfiletoc.htm

Thomas, C. (2004). How is disability understood? An examination of sociological approaches. *Disability and Society, 19*(6), 569–583.

Thornton, M., & Downs, S. (2010). Walking the walk: Social model and universal design in the disabilities office. *Journal of Postsecondary Education and Disability, 23*(1), 74–80.

United Nations Enable. (2006). *Preamble to the Convention on the Rights of Persons with Disabilities.* Retrieved from http://www.un.org/disabilities/default.asp?id=260

Wunder, G. (2013). Ten million books and counting. *Braille Monitor, 56*(1). Retrieved from https://nfb.org/images/nfb/publications/bm/bm13/bm1301/bm130102.htm

World Health Organization. (2011). *World report on disability.* Retrieved from http://whqlibdoc. who.int/hq/2011/WHO_NMH_VIP_11.01_eng.pdf

Chapter 3

Universal Design in Higher Education

Sheryl Burgstahler

P ostsecondary institutions are required by law (Section 504 of the Rehabilitation Act of 1973 and the Americans with Disabilities Act of 1990 and its 2008 amendments) to provide access to courses, technology, and services for qualified students with disabilities. When an educational product or environment is not fully accessible, institutions must extend reasonable accommodations to those who disclose their disabilities and present appropriate documentation. Despite strong civil

This chapter is based on work supported by the National Science Foundation (grant # CNS-1042260, HRD-0833504, HRD-0929006). Any opinions, findings, and conclusions or recommendations are those of the author and do not necessarily reflect the policy or views of the National Science Foundation, and the reader should not assume its endorsement.

rights legislation in the United States and increasing numbers of people with disabilities attending colleges and universities, a significant gap exists in the achievement of postsecondary degrees for students with disabilities compared with their peers without disabilities (Belch, 2004; National Council on Disability, 2003; Wagner, Newman, Cameto, & Levine, 2005). Success stories demonstrate that opportunities do exist for students with disabilities who successfully overcome barriers imposed by inaccessible facilities, curricula, websites, technology, and student services; insufficient accommodations and supports; and others' low expectations, as well as inadequate skills in self-advocacy and lack of access to role models and peers with disabilities (Disabilities, Opportunities, Internetworking, and Technology [DO-IT], 1993–2012; Stern & Woods, 2001).

Student Retention

Researchers and practitioners have identified factors that affect student retention at both the individual (e.g., socioeconomic status) and institutional (e.g., policies, procedures) levels (Braxton, Sullivan, & Johnson, 1997; Tinto, 1993). Berge and Huang (2004) encourage institutions to consider the interconnectivities among personal and institutional factors, which can lead to interventions that:

- Encourage commitment on the part of individuals and the institution.
- Enhance integration.
- Improve delivery systems.
- Increase person-environmental fit.
- Improve outcomes.

Consistent with this approach, researchers and practitioners have recommended interventions for both students and institutions to reduce the gap in postsecondary success between students with and without disabilities along these lines:

- Students with disabilities should develop self-determination skills so they can effectively advocate for reasonable accommodations and otherwise be better prepared to succeed in the college environment (Getzel & Thoma, 2008).
- Postsecondary institutions should make their physical environments, technology, services, and courses more welcoming and accessible to students with disabilities (Burgstahler, 2008a).

Many efforts to assist postsecondary students with disabilities focus on the "deficit" of the individual and on making accommodations so that he or she can fit into an established environment. In contrast (as Jean Ashmore and Devva Kasnitz describe in Chapter 2), the social model of disability and other integrated approaches in the field of disability studies view variations in abilities—like those with respect to gender, race, and ethnicity—as a natural part of the human experience; therefore, all products and environments should be designed with diversity in abilities in mind.

Universal Design in Higher Education

Universal design (UD) challenges the common practice of designing products and environments for the average user by promoting consideration of a wide range of characteristics, including disabilities. Institutions employ both proactive and reactive approaches to address access issues. An example of a reactive approach is providing, upon request, a sign language interpreter as an accommodation in a meeting attended by a student who is deaf. Most people would agree that it would be unreasonable to hire sign language interpreters to be present in all classes and all meetings, just in case a student who would benefit from the interpretation shows up. However, there are other situations in which being proactive in dealing with accessibility issues is practical and can reduce or even eliminate the need for individual accommodations. UD is appropriate in these cases.

Ronald Mace—an internationally recognized architect and educator—coined the term *universal design* in the 1970s. Through the

Center for Universal Design (CUD) at North Carolina State University, Mace defined UD as "the design of products and environments to be usable by all people, to the greatest extent possible, without the need for adaptation or specialized design" (CUD, n.d., para. 1). An example of UD is integrating a wheelchair-accessible entrance into the overall design of a building, thus benefiting people who are using walkers or wheelchairs, people pushing baby strollers or delivery carts, and those whose health conditions make walking up and down steps difficult.

Universal Design of Instruction

Studies of learning styles, strengths, and preferences of students have revealed that students have a wide variety of preferred learning modes, including auditory, visual, tactile, and kinesthetic styles (Wooldridge, 1995); experience learning according to their dominant styles as a converger, diverger, accommodator, or assimilator (Svinicki & Dixon, 1987); and perceive the world in ways that include linguistic, logical-mathematical, spatial, bodily-kinesthetic, musical, interpersonal, intrapersonal, and naturalistic (Gardner, 1983). Educators who embrace UD employ a mix of teaching approaches to address the expected learning differences of their students. They may use multiple modes for the delivery of content (e.g., lectures, videos, readings, discussions); multiple ways for students to interact with each other (e.g., on-site, online); and multiple ways for students to demonstrate what they have learned (e.g., projects, written exam items in various formats). They can then apply UD in the implementation of each method selected. For example, an instructor could apply UD to small group discussions by ensuring that all participants are engaged and to lectures by verbally describing the content presented in visuals.

The level of UD application can be viewed on a continuum. Posting class notes on a website provides a benefit to most students, but sharing these materials in a format that is accessible to students who are blind and using searchable screen reader technology demonstrates a deeper application of UD. In short, an instructor who adopts a UD philosophy is never finished, but rather is always exploring ways to make a course more inclusive of everyone (Burgstahler, 2011).

Some researchers and practitioners have identified UD strategies that have a foundation in research or practice. They have documented UD practices to include captions on videos; handouts provided in alternative formats; presentation visuals with large, bold fonts and high-contrast, uncluttered backgrounds; adjustments to the physical environment to accommodate wheelchairs; Internet-based distance learning courses that apply accessibility guidelines; and instructor behaviors that make presentations accessible, such as describing orally all content that is presented in visuals, avoiding unnecessary jargon, defining terms that might be unfamiliar to some attendees, and providing students with scaffolding devices; and engaging the audience in multiple ways (Bruch, 2003; Burgstahler & Doe, 2006; Burgstahler, 2011; Cunningham, 2003; Gradel & Edson, 2009–2010; Harrison, 2006; Johnson & Fox, 2003; Mason & Orkwis, 2005; McAlexander, 2003; Mino, 2004; Moriarty, 2007; Ouellett, 2004; Pieper, 2005; Pliner & Johnson, 2004; Rose, Harbour, Johnston, Dadye, & Abarbannel, 2006; Scott, McGuire, & Shaw, 2003; Silver, Bourke, & Strehorn, 1998).

From this rich literature base, collaborators in projects funded by the U.S. Department of Education (DO-IT, 2012) at the DO-IT Center at the University of Washington developed guidelines for applying UD to instruction (Burgstahler, 2008b). Draft checklists were created and, in an informal iterative process, experiences in applying strategies from the checklist on more than 20 campuses led to modifications. The checklist offers educators a good place to start integrating UD into all aspects of their instruction. It includes the following:

- *Class climate.* Adopt practices that reflect high values with respect to both diversity and inclusiveness.
- *Interaction.* Encourage regular and effective interactions between students and the instructor, and ensure that communication methods are accessible for all participants.

- *Physical environments/products.* Ensure that facilities, activities, materials, and equipment are physically accessible to and usable by all students, and that all potential student characteristics are addressed in safety considerations.
- *Delivery methods.* Use multiple instructional methods that are accessible for all learners.
- *Information resources/technology.* Ensure that course materials, notes, and other information resources are engaging, flexible, and accessible for all students.
- *Feedback.* Provide specific feedback on a regular basis.
- *Assessment.* Regularly assess student progress using multiple accessible methods and tools, and adjust instruction accordingly.
- *Accommodation plan.* Provide accommodations for students whose needs are not met by the instructional design. (Burgstahler, 2008b)

The largest collection of research papers that support UD instructional practices was compiled at the Center for Applied Special Technology (CAST, n.d.). With studies in neuroscience, cognitive neuroscience, and neuropsychology as a research basis, researchers constructed a general framework for universal design for learning (UDL), suggesting that educators provide students with multiple means of representation, action and expression, and engagement. Through a meta-analysis of available research studies, UDL researchers identified effective teaching practices and organized them around the three principles of UDL. Most of the articles are about education at the K–12 level, focus on reading and writing skills, and relate to a very specific strategy and setting.

Research that compares the results of postsecondary courses taught with and without the application of UD strategies is beginning to emerge in the literature. For example, Beckman (2009) reported that when two versions of a graduate information management course were offered—one section taught in the way it had been offered in the past and one taught with the addition of small group discussions—students in the section with small group discussions said they perceived that the instructor was open to a variety of points of view more often than did students in the other section. In exams, the students in the UD section performed better on essay questions, but both groups performed the same on multiple-choice/ fill-in-the-blank questions.

Student outcomes from faculty training in UD were assessed in the DO-IT project described above (DO-IT, 2009). Specifically, using a quasi-experimental 2x2 research design, student course grades were collected at two points in time—before the training was offered ("pre") and after the training was offered ("post")—in classes taught by faculty who received UD training and in classes taught by matched faculty who did not receive training. The grades of students with disabilities in classes taught by faculty who received training increased more than the grades of those in courses taught by untrained faculty, whereas the performance of students without disabilities stayed about the same. The performance of students with and without disabilities was close to the same level after instructors were trained in UD. Students with disabilities have also reported that they benefit from a wide range of UD strategies (Durre, Richardson, Smith, Shulman, & Steele, 2008; Kortering, McClannon, & Braziel, 2005) and that faculty trained in UD applications actually employ them in their courses (Schelly, Davies, & Spooner, 2004).

The UD approach has been supported in federal legislation. For example, the Higher Education Opportunity Act of 2008 promotes the application of UD and other strategies and the creation of corresponding resources for faculty and administrators that can help them make postsecondary education more accessible to students with disabilities (Gordon, Gravel, & Schifter, 2009). Universal design of instruction has been embraced by growing numbers of faculty and administrators (e.g., Burgstahler & Doe, 2006; Gordon et al., 2009; Harrison, 2006; Ouellett, 2004; Shaw & Scott, 2003) and by some professional organizations, such as the Association on Higher Education and Disability (AHEAD, n.d.). Across the country, some on-site and online professional development offerings for faculty promote UD as a best practice and provide useful guidelines (e.g., AHEAD, n.d.; Darr & Jones, 2008; DO-IT, n.d.; Getzel, Briel, & McManus, 2003; Gradel & Edison, 2009–2010).

Universal Design of Student Services

Student services (e.g., residential services, computer labs, career centers) play important roles in the success of students. Various authors have discussed accessibility challenges to services: Anderson et al., 2008; Burgstahler, 2008c; Burgstahler & Moore, 2009; Higbee & Eaton, 2003; Schmetzke, 2002; Uzes & Connelly, 2003; and Wisbey & Kalivoda, 2003. In one study (Burgstahler & Moore, 2009), students with disabilities shared their perceptions regarding the knowledge, skills, and attitudes of student service personnel. Although many comments were positive, some students reported that staff members did not understand their need for accommodations; lacked knowledge regarding invisible disabilities; and made comments that reflected disrespect or impatience. Both staff and students with disabilities made suggestions for improving student services; for example, offering multiple service counter heights and designing online resources to be accessible. In another project hosted by the DO-IT Center (Burgstahler, 2008c), collaborators developed a draft UD checklist that was further validated and fine-tuned with results from a nationwide survey. Available online, the checklist covers the following application areas:

- *Planning, policies, and evaluation.* Consider diversity issues, including those related to disability, as you plan and evaluate services.
- *Physical environments and products.* Ensure physical access, comfort, and safety in an environment that is inclusive of people with a variety of abilities, racial and ethnic backgrounds, genders, and ages.
- *Staff.* Make sure staff are prepared to work with all students.
- *Information resources and technology.* If your service unit uses computers as information resources, ensure that these systems

employ accessibility options and that systems are in place to make accommodations.

- *Events.* Ensure that everyone can participate in events sponsored by your organization. (p. 171)

Implications for Practice

Applying the UD approach holds promise for making academic programs and services welcoming and accessible to all students, including those with disabilities. However, driving systemic change can be difficult, time-consuming, and messy. A person who is serious about pursuing this path should be prepared to be a disruptive innovator, where "your job is a platform. It's not just a job, it's a way for you to inspire others and create things. . . . You're not afraid of the path less traveled . . . " (Ideablendedu, n.d., para. 1). To engage with others who have similar interests, early adopters should consider joining the online Universal Design in Higher Education community of practice by sending a request to doit@uw.edu. To move toward a more universally designed campus, institutions should consider creating a task force or advisory board to review current policies and practices and take steps or make recommendations to ensure the following:

- Vision, mission, and value statements of the institution, academic units, and services reflect a high value on diversity defined broadly and on addressing issues relevant to students with disabilities.
- Teaching and student service practices (with respect to planning, policies, and evaluation; physical environments and products; staff; information resources and technology; and events) are selected and designed to meet the needs of all students, especially students with disabilities.
- Data collection and reporting routines reflect high priorities with respect to diversity, thus including information relevant to students with disabilities.
- UD professional development is provided to faculty and staff.

Conclusion

The increasingly diverse student body on postsecondary campuses includes growing numbers of students with disabilities. To make their offerings more inclusive, institutions should ensure that policies and practices reflect a high value for diversity of all types. Originally applied to the development of physical spaces, technology, and consumer products, UD has recently emerged as a paradigm for the development of instruction and student services. This approach benefits many students and reduces the need for disability-related accommodations. Implementation of UD may contribute to reducing the gap that persists in the achievement of postsecondary degrees for students with and without disabilities.

References

ADA Amendments Act of 2008, 42 U.S.C. § 12101 note (2011).

Americans with Disabilities Act of 1990, 42 U.S.C., § 12101 *et seq.* (2011).

Anderson, A., Cory, R. C., Griffin, P., Richter, P. J., Ferguson, S., Patterson, E., & Reed, L. (2008). Applications of universal design to student services: Experiences in the field. In S. Burgstahler & R. Cory (Eds.), *Universal design in higher education: From principles to practice* (pp. 177–186). Cambridge, MA: Harvard Education Press.

Association on Higher Education and Disability. (n.d.). *Universal design.* Retrieved from http://www.ahead.org/resources/universal-design

Beckman, P. (2009). Universal design for learning: A field experiment comparing specific classroom actions (AMCIS 2009 Proceedings Paper No. 10). Retrieved from http://aisel.aisnet.org/amcis2009/10

Belch, H. A. (2004). Retention and students with disabilities. *Journal of College Student Retention: Research, Theory, & Practice, 6*(1), 3–22.

Berge, Z. L., & Huang, Y. (2004). A model for sustainable student retention: A holistic perspective on the student dropout problem with special attention to e-learning. *DEOSNEWS, 13*(5). Retrieved from http://www.ed.psu.edu/acsde/deos/deosnews/deosnews13_5.pdf

Braxton, J. M., Sullivan, A. V., & Johnson, R. M. (1997). Appraising Tinto's theory of college student departure. In J. C. Smart (Ed.), *Higher education: Handbook of theory and research* (Vol. XII, pp. 107–164). New York, NY: Agathon.

Bruch, P. L. (2003). Interpreting and implementing universal instructional design in basic writing. In J. Higbee (Ed.), *Curriculum transformation and disability: Implementing universal design in higher education* (pp. 93–103). Minneapolis, MN: University of Minnesota, Center for Research on Developmental Education and Urban Literacy.

Burgstahler, S. (2008a). Universal design in higher education. In S. Burgstahler & R. Cory (Eds.), *Universal design in higher education: From principles to practice* (pp. 3–20). Cambridge, MA: Harvard Education Press.

Burgstahler, S. (2008b). Universal design of instruction: From principles to practice. In S. Burgstahler & R. Cory (Eds.), *Universal design in higher education: From principles to practice* (pp. 23–43). Cambridge, MA: Harvard Education Press.

Burgstahler, S. (2008c). Universal design of student services: From principles to practice. In S. Burgstahler & R. Cory (Eds.), *Universal design in higher education: From principles to practice* (pp. 167–175). Cambridge, MA: Harvard Education Press.

Burgstahler, S. (2011). Universal design: Implications for computing education. *ACM Transactions on Computing Education, 11*(3). Retrieved from http://staff.washington.edu/sherylb/ud_computing.html

Burgstahler, S., & Doe, T. (2006). Improving postsecondary outcomes for students with disabilities: Designing professional development for faculty. *Journal of Postsecondary Education and Disability, 18*(2), 135–147.

Burgstahler, S., & Moore, E. (2009). Making student services welcoming and accessible through accommodations and universal design. *Journal of Postsecondary Education and Disability, 21*(3), 151–174.

Center for Applied Special Technology. (n.d.). *UDL guidelines–Version 1.0: Research evidence.* Retrieved from http://www.udlcenter.org/aboutudl/udlguidelines

Center for Universal Design. (n.d.) *About UD.* Retrieved from http://www.ncsu.edu/ncsu/design/cud/about_ud/about_ud.htm

Cunningham, A. (2003). Supporting student-centered teaching and learning: Technology in Wake Forest University education programs. *Contemporary Issues in Technology and Teacher Education, 3*(1), 57–70.

Darr, A., & Jones, R. (2008). The contribution of universal design to learning and teaching excellence. In S. Burgstahler & R. Cory (Eds.), *Universal design in higher education: From principles to practice* (pp. 105–108). Cambridge, MA: Harvard Education Press.

Disabilities, Opportunities, Internetworking, and Technology. (n.d.). *Center for Universal Design in Education.* Retrieved from http://www.washington.edu/doit/CUDE

Disabilities, Opportunities, Internetworking, and Technology. (1993–2012). *DO-IT snapshots.* Retrieved from http://www.washington.edu/doit/Snapshots

Disabilities, Opportunities, Internetworking, and Technology. (2009). *Final report of the AccessCollege project to the Office of Postsecondary Education, U. S. Department of Education.* Seattle, WA: University of Washington.

Disabilities, Opportunities, Internetworking, and Technology. (2012). *AccessCollege: Systemic change for postsecondary institutions.* Retrieved from http://www.washington.edu/doit/Brochures/Academics/access_college.html

Durre, I., Richardson, M., Smith, C., Shulman, J. A., & Steele, S. (2008). Universal design of instruction: Reflections of students. In S. Burgstahler & R. Cory (Eds.), *Universal design in higher education: From principles to practice* (pp. 83–96). Cambridge, MA: Harvard Education Press.

Gardner, H. (1983). *Frames of mind: The theory of multiple intelligences.* New York, NY: Basic Books.

Getzel, E. E., Briel, L. W., & McManus, S. (2003). Strategies for implementing professional development activities on college campuses: Findings from the OPE-funded project sites (1999-2002). *Journal of Postsecondary Education and Disability, 17*(1), 59–78.

Getzel, E. E., & Thoma, C. A. (2008). Experiences of college students with disabilities and the importance of self-determination in higher education. *Career Development and Transition for Exceptional Individuals, 31*(2), 77–84.

Gordon, D. T., Gravel, J. W., & Schifter, L. A. (Eds.). (2009). *A policy reader in universal design for learning.* Cambridge, MA: Harvard Education Press.

Gradel, K., & Edson, A. (2009–2010). Putting universal design for learning on the higher ed agenda. *Journal of Educational Technology Systems, 38*(2), 111–121.

Harrison, E. G. (2006). Working with faculty toward universally designed instruction: The process of dynamic course design. *Journal of Postsecondary Education and Disability, 19*(2), 152–162.

Higbee, J. L., & Eaton, S. B. (2003). Implementing universal design in learning centers. In J. Higbee (Ed.), *Curriculum transformation and disability: Implementing universal design in higher education* (pp. 215–230). Minneapolis, MN: University of Minnesota, Center for Research on Developmental Education and Urban Literacy.

Higher Education Opportunity Act of 2008, 20 U.S.C. § 1001 note (2012).

Ideablendedu. (n.d.). *15 ways you know you are a disruptive innovator in higher education.* Idea Blend EDU. Retrieved from http://ideablendedu.org/innovative-professional-development/15-ways-you-know-you-are-a-disruptive-innovator-in-higher-education

Johnson, D. M., & Fox, J. A. (2003). Creating curb cuts in the classroom: Adapting universal design principles to education. In J. Higbee (Ed.), *Curriculum transformation and disability: Implementing universal design in higher education* (pp. 7–22). Minneapolis, MN: University of Minnesota, Center for Research on Developmental Education and Urban Literacy.

Kortering, L., McClannon, T., & Braziel, P. (2005). What algebra and biology students have to say about universal design for learning. *National Center for Secondary Education and Transition Research to Practice Brief, 4*(2). Retrieved from http://www.ncset.org/publications/viewdesc.asp?id=2568

Mason, C., & Orkwis, R. (2005). Instructional theories supporting universal design for learning— Teaching to individual learners. In Council for Exceptional Children (Ed.), *Universal design for learning: A guide for teachers and education professionals* (pp. 21–39). Upper Saddle River, NJ: Pearson Prentice Hall.

McAlexander, P. J. (2003). Using principles of universal design in college composition courses. In J. Higbee (Ed.), *Curriculum transformation and disability: Implementing universal design in higher education* (pp. 105–114). Minneapolis, MN: University of Minnesota, Center for Research on Developmental Education and Urban Literacy.

Mino, J. (2004). Planning for inclusion: Using universal instructional design to create a learner-centered community college classroom. *Equity and Excellence in Education, 37*(2), 154–160.

Moriarty, M. A. (2007). Inclusive pedagogy: Teaching methodologies to reach diverse learners in science instruction. *Equity and Excellence in Education, 40*(3), 252–265.

National Council on Disability. (2003). *People with disabilities and postsecondary education— position paper.* Retrieved from http://www.ncd.gov/publications/2003/Sept152003

Ouellett, M. L. (2004). Faculty development and universal instructional design. *Equity and Excellence in Education, 37*, 135–144.

Pieper, M. (2005). Digital divide and learning disabilities—Counteracting educational exclusion in information society. *ACM SIGACCESS Accessibility and Computing, 83*, 37–41.

Pliner, S., & Johnson, J. (2004). Historical, theoretical, and foundational principles of universal instructional design in higher education. *Equity and Excellence in Education, 37*, 105–113.

Rehabilitation Act of 1973 §504, 29 U.S.C. § 794 (2012).

Rose, D. H., Harbour, W. S., Johnson, C. S., Dadye, S. G., & Abarbannel, I. (2006). Universal design for learning in postsecondary education: Reflections and principles and their applications. *Journal of Postsecondary Education and Disability, 19*(2), 135–151.

47

Schelly, C. L., Davies, P. L., & Spooner, C. L. (2004). Student perceptions of faculty implementation of universal design for learning. *Journal of Postsecondary Education and Disability, 24*(1), 17–30. Retrieved from http://accessproject.colostate.edu/assets/PDFs/Schelly,%20Davies,%20Spooner%202011.pdf

Schmetzke, A. (2002). Web accessibility at university libraries and library schools. *Library Hi Tech, 19*(1), 35–49.

Scott, S., McGuire, J., & Shaw, S. (2003). Universal design for instruction: A new paradigm for adult instruction in postsecondary education. *Remedial and Special Education, 24*(6), 369–379.

Shaw, S. F., & Scott, S. S. 2003. New directions in faculty development. *Journal of Postsecondary Education and Disability, 17*(1), 3–9.

Silver, P., Bourke, A., & Strehorn, K. C. (1998). Universal instructional design in higher education: An approach for inclusion. *Equity and Excellence in Education, 31*(2), 47–51.

Stern, V., & Woods, M. (2001). *Roadmaps and rampways.* Washington, DC: American Association for the Advancement of Science.

Svinicki, M. D., & Dixon, N. M. (1987). The Kolb model modified for classroom activities. *College Teaching, 35,* 141–146.

Tinto, V. (1993). *Leaving college: Rethinking the causes and cures of student attrition* (2nd ed.). Chicago, IL: University of Chicago Press.

Uzes, K. B., & Connelly, D. (2003). Universal design in counseling center service areas. In J. Higbee (Ed.), *Curriculum transformation and disability: Implementing universal design in higher education* (pp. 241–250). Minneapolis, MN: University of Minnesota, Center for Research on Developmental Education and Urban Literacy.

Wagner, M., Newman, L., Cameto, R., & Levine, P. (2005). *Changes over time in the early postschool outcomes of youth with disabilities: A report of findings from the National Longitudinal Transition Study (NLTS) and the National Longitudinal Transition Study-2 (NLTS2).* Menlo Park, CA: SRI International.

Wisbey, M. E., & Kalivoda, K. S. (2003). Residential living for all: Fully accessible and "livable" on-campus housing. In J. Higbee (Ed.), *Curriculum transformation and disability: Implementing universal design in higher education* (pp. 241–250). Minneapolis, MN: University of Minnesota: Center for Research on Developmental Education and Urban Literacy.

Wooldridge, B. (1995). Increasing the effectiveness of university/college instruction: The results of learning style research into course design and delivery. In R. R. Sims, & S. J. Sims (Eds.), *The importance of learning styles* (pp. 49–68). Westport, CT: Greenwood Press.

PART II

Information and Communication Technology

Chapter 4

Accessible Technology in Student Affairs

Rachel Luna

"It is unacceptable for universities to use emerging technology without insisting that this technology be accessible to all students." —U.S. Department of Justice and U.S. Department of Education, Joint *Dear Colleague* Letter, 2010, para. 5

In the 21st century, the adage "meeting students where they are" increasingly means meeting them via technology, often via social media. But this advancement is not without potential pitfalls in the realm of accessibility. For example, an inspirational video shared on a university's Facebook page might help some students stay motivated during finals, but if it does not include captions or audio descriptions, students with hearing or vision impairments will not be as well supported. Or a LinkedIn group for alumni members that precludes those with visual impairments from connecting with other community members because the login requires a CAPTCHA (an image used to verify human users). Or an instant messenger client for office hours that is an efficient way to respond to advising queries, but is difficult for students who have color blindness to use because they cannot distinguish between the green "I'm available" and the red "Do not disturb" icons.

Technology-mediated spaces (e.g., websites, applications, social networks) are extensions of the campus environment and have the potential to affect members of the community in positive or negative ways. Strange (2000) described a hierarchy of learning environments wherein the lowest level provides safety and inclusion, with basic feelings of security and belonging; the next level includes involvement and engagement; and the highest level is full membership in the community. If technology is used to create higher education environments without proper regard to accessibility, students with disabilities are left with no pathways to get to higher levels. Electronic accessibility barriers can affect the success and persistence of students with disabilities. As student affairs professionals continue to adopt and use emerging technologies, they must also adapt and respond to emerging accessibility challenges to remain inclusive, legally compliant, and socially just.

This chapter offers a context for why accessibility is mandatory when using technology, an overview of technology use in student affairs and its related challenges, examples of guidelines and benchmarks for achieving accessibility, and resources for accessible practice.

Laws and Litigation

Under U.S. law, accessibility for people with disabilities is more than a strong suggestion; it is a mandate. Although many of these regulations predate the birth of current technologies, government offices have consistently confirmed that accessibility principles are applicable to newer technologies. In addition, contemporary interpretations by the courts and revisions of standards ensure that these policies remain relevant amidst technological advances.

Both Section 504 of the Rehabilitation Act of 1973 and the Americans with Disabilities Act of 1990 were written before widespread Internet availability and use. Nevertheless, the U.S. Department of Justice and the U.S. Department of Education Office for Civil Rights have affirmed the application of both laws to the Internet and computer technologies (U.S. Department of Justice, 1996; U.S. Department of Education, 1996). In 1998, Section 508 was added to the Rehabilitation Act to specifically address technology accessibility by establishing requirements for electronic information technology from the federal government.

The U.S. Department of Justice has supported technology and accessibility in higher education by responding to lawsuits and formal civil rights complaints against a handful of universities for using inaccessible technologies that discriminate against students with visual impairments. These technologies have included electronic book readers (U.S. Department of Justice, 2009a, 2009b, 2010a, 2010b) and Internet-based learning environments (U.S. Department of Justice, 2013). The courts have said that mandatory accessibility is not limited to college or university campuses. In 2011, the Law School Admissions Council signed an agreement with the National Federation of the Blind and the U.S. Department of Justice to make the council's website and its functions accessible to people who use screen readers in time for the fall 2012 admissions cycle (U.S. Department of Justice, 2011). Victories and settlements create strong legal precedent and solidly establish accessibility as a requirement in higher education.

Technology Accessibility Challenges

The World Wide Web Consortium (2005) offered a definition of web accessibility that says, "People with disabilities can perceive, understand, navigate, and interact with the Web, and . . . they can contribute to the Web" (para. 1). In this definition, disabilities can include auditory, visual, physical, cognitive, and neurological impairments. Although the definition is focused on Internet use, the principles of accessibility can be expanded to include other forms of technology.

As a profession, student affairs uses a plethora of technologies (websites, organization management systems, student information databases, etc.). In recent years, social media have become popular and prevalent forms of technology in higher education and student affairs work, and this growth will continue. In a 2011 study at the University of Massachusetts, Dartmouth, 100% of the colleges and universities studied used some form of social media (Barnes & Lescault, 2011).

Facebook was reported as the most popular social network not only among higher education institutions in the United States (98%) but also among the overall national population (Barnes & Lescault, 2011; Nielsen, 2012). The professional social network LinkedIn is rising in popularity in higher education settings, with 47% of schools reporting using LinkedIn in functional areas such as career centers, admissions offices, and alumni relations. Unfortunately, both of these networks present a variety of accessibility challenges (Bordeau, 2011; Media Access Australia, 2011). For example, Facebook and LinkedIn both use CAPTCHA image technology to verify that users are not robots, and both have navigation structures that can be challenging for screen readers and keyboard navigation.

- *Video, images, and multimedia content.* YouTube had the next highest reported rates of use in higher education at 86% (Barnes & Lescault, 2011). The main accessibility issue with this site, and similar use of videos or other multimedia content, is caption support for people with hearing impairments (Media Access Australia, 2011). YouTube has increased feasibility for users to add their own transcripts and captions and has made improvements in providing basic autocaptioning. However, not all social media video sites offer the same accessibility functions (e.g., Vimeo does not currently support captioning). Image-based media such as Instagram (a photo-sharing application) and Pinterest (an online pinboard) have surged in popularity in recent years. These media offer interesting and creative opportunities for campus community-building. However, they present new and continuing accessibility challenges. Students with visual impairments can find it hard to fully engage in the environments of multimedia programs that rely on user-generated submissions for captions and descriptive text.

- *Blogs and microblogs.* Blog sites (such as those powered by WordPress) and microblog sites (such as Twitter) have high adoption rates in higher education and powerful potential for storytelling, but they do not always include accessibility features (Barnes & Lescault, 2011). Common accessibility issues plaguing blogs and microblog sites are related to navigation and readability (Media Access Australia, 2011), which can drive users with disabilities to other sites. For example, they might use the more accessible Easy Chirp instead of the native Twitter website.

- *Third-party applications.* More colleges are using third-party applications for technology services such as campus e-mail, calendars, and cloud-based storage, and Google is one of the leaders in this area (Young, 2012). This can be a cost-effective and efficient option for campus information technology departments, but it is not without accessibility concerns. A report from the Access Technology Higher Education Network (ATHEN, 2012) detailed accessibility concerns with certain Gmail and Google Calendar functions. The NFB has filed multiple complaints against colleges and universities that use or plan to use the Google Apps for Education suite.

Emerging Challenges

New technologies are developed and adopted by higher education institutions every day, and student affairs professionals must keep up with the constant change. Two examples of emerging technologies that could present accessibility challenges are massive open online courses (MOOCs) and mobile technology.

- *Massive open online courses.* The 2013 *Horizon Report* for higher education described MOOCs as evolving "at an unprecedented pace" (Johnson et al., 2013, p. 11). This reimagination of distance education consists of classes offered via websites free or at little cost to large numbers of students. As educators struggle to figure out how to teach on such a large scale, student affairs professionals may be called upon to figure out how to ensure accessibility on the same large scale.
- *Mobile technology.* According to *The Chronicle of Higher Education* (2012), colleges and universities of all institutional types are increasing their mobile capabilities. *The Chronicle* found that the most popular mobile services are focused on students, including learning/course management systems, library services, and student recruitment and admissions. As institutions adapt to the student demand for more mobile services, student affairs professionals must ensure the accessibility of these applications for all members of the community, including people with disabilities.

Because change is constant, so must be the commitment to accessibility. As technology continues to change, how will student affairs professionals keep up with accessibility? Adhering to overarching universal design principles and intentional planning processes will allow higher education professionals to maintain high standards of accessibility even as the media continue to change.

Taking Action

Accessibility must be addressed from a variety of perspectives if it is to be supported and sustained in student affairs technology. Widespread awareness and understanding of universal design (UD) principles can serve as a foundation for accessibility. An overall philosophy of inclusion will drive development and implementation of organizational accessibility plans.

Applying Universal Design Principles to Student Affairs Technology

UD consists of seven principles: (1) equitable use, (2) flexibility in use, (3) simple and intuitive use, (4) perceptible information, (5) tolerance for error, (6) low physical effort, and (7) size and space for approach and use (Center for Universal Design, 1997). Student affairs professionals can apply these principles to their work with technology and can implement inclusive policies and practices to create welcoming and accessible higher education environments. For example, UD principles can be applied to the computer kiosks that are available in many student services offices by allowing for height adjustment options to accommodate users with mobility or size issues and by providing a trackball pointing device to accommodate users who cannot use a traditional mouse. Providing materials in multiple media formats and languages also enhances universal accessibility. Another example of UD principles in action can be found at colleges and universities that have made navigating campus environments easier for everyone with detailed maps and building diagrams (Boston University, n.d.; Colorado College, n.d.; University of Alaska Anchorage, 2012; Western University, 2013).

For more examples and resources, publications from the PASS IT (Pedagogy and Student Services for Institutional Transformation) project at the University of Minnesota explore applications of UD concepts in various higher education environments (Higbee & Goff, 2008). PASS IT guidebooks offer resources for applying UD principles for student development programs and services, including scenarios and implementation tools. The DO-IT (Disabilities, Opportunities, Internetworking, and Technology) program at the University of Washington (UW) also explains UD applications in specific student services areas such as advising, financial aid, and student organizations (UW, 2013). DO-IT offers checklists, guidelines, and information on resources, technology, and other topics, such as physical environment and staff.

Gaining Online Accessible Learning through Self-Study (GOALS)

For implementing and institutionalizing widespread change, Project GOALS from the National Center on Disability and Access to Education (NCDAE) (2011) provides a self-assessment tool, a persuasive action paper, and resources for creating action plans. According to GOALS, the following four indicators reflect overall institutional commitment to Web accessibility:

- *Institutional vision and leadership commitment.* The first indicator of Web accessibility is the commitment of administrative leadership (e.g., an articulated vision statement or creation of a task force) and participation of other relevant stakeholders, including students, staff, and faculty (e.g., offering opportunities for feedback and professional development).
- *Planning and implementation.* Next, GOALS calls for strategic planning to support and maintain Web accessibility. In the planning process, benchmarks exist for including key personnel in all phases of planning (including policy development and implementation), developing a comprehensive accessibility policy (including technical standards and provisions for procurement), writing the accessibility plan (including seeking and using campuswide feedback), and implementing the written plan (including training personnel and tracking implementation progress).
- *Resources and support.* The third GOALS indicator stresses the importance of adequate resources and support for Web accessibility, which begins with a focus on hiring and supporting personnel who can help achieve accessibility goals. However, the presence of these personnel is not sufficient to sustain accessibility efforts; the personnel need enough time and energy to be effective. Other key benchmarks in this area are budget allocation

and ensuring that feedback is used to determine allocation of funds. The final benchmarks are related to training, supporting, developing, and using the technologies that help make content accessible.

- *Assessment.* The final part of the GOALS self-study tool describes good practice for assessment to measure progress and make ongoing improvements. Formal communications about the implementation process are prime opportunities to invite direct feedback from students with disabilities and provide evidence for evaluating progress. In addition, reports focusing on Web accessibility outcomes can indicate whether efforts are meeting intended goals. Finally, the assessment data collected should be used to inform and improve institutional efforts.

Figure 4.1 summarizes the GOALS indicators and benchmarks. For more detailed descriptions and specific examples of recommended indicators, go to the NCDAE website (www.ncdae.org, 2011).

Web Content Accessibility Guidelines 2.0

Whereas the GOALS initiative provides a big-picture perspective on implementing change at an institution, the Web Content Accessibility Guidelines (WCAG) 2.0 provide more specific and tangible guidelines for the technological environment and its structure (websites, user interactions, etc.). Developed by the World Wide Web Consortium (W3), WCAG 2.0 is a set of recommendations for making web content more accessible (W3, 2012). The recommendations are set forth in 12 guidelines, each with three testable success levels: A, AA, and AAA.

These guidelines are based on four principles of accessibility: perceivable, operable, understandable, and robust (POUR).The *perceivable* principle seeks to ensure that Web users have feasible access to content using the abilities they have (i.e., text alternatives such as captions). Success in the *operable* principle means that users can control the functions of the website, particularly with the keyboard. The third accessibility principle requires content to be *understandable*, which means not using jargon and having a predictable and consistent website structure. *Robust* is the final accessibility principle; it calls for compatibility with current and future user agents, especially with assistive technologies.

The W3C website is a rich repository of resources for understanding and implementing the standards of this global initiative, including explanations for every provision in the document and suggested techniques for success criteria at all levels. For a summary of WCAG 2.0, see Figure 4.2.

There is no official global Web accessibility standard, but WCAG 2.0 is at the forefront of the movement. As of 1999, most Section 508 standards were consistent with Level A of WCAG 1.0 and action is being taken to harmonize these standards with Levels A and AA of WCAG 2.0. Although adoption of standards is becoming more common in the public sector, compliance elsewhere is lagging. In 2011, a review of popular social media sites found low success ratings for WCAG 2.0 compliance (Bordeau, 2011). Five social media sites were reviewed and none scored higher than 29%. Higher education websites have similarly poor WCAG 2.0 compliance. A survey of websites at 20 universities that have Web accessibility policies found that 80% had accessibility errors on the home page and 77% had accessibility errors on other pages (WebAIM, 2013a).

Promising Practices and Additional Resources

Higher education institutions throughout the country can offer plenty of positive examples of accessibility in practice. For example, Pennsylvania State University (PSU), once a target of an NFB complaint, now has a vibrant accessibility website with resources and tools for students, staff, and faculty (PSU, 2012). The California State University (CSU) system launched the Accessible Technology Initiative in 2005; it provides resources including manual evaluation tools, "From Where I Sit" videos, transcripts of experiences of students with disabilities, and a collaborative Center for Accessible Media (CSU, Office of the Chancellor, n.d.). WebAIM (Web Accessibility In Mind) an initiative affiliated with Utah State University, offers a variety of resources for complying with and testing for accessibility standards, including a Web accessibility evaluation tool (WAVE) for use in conducting self-audits of websites and code samples; checklists for interpreting and complying with Section 508 and WCAG 2.0 standards; and explanatory videos on Web accessibility (WebAIM, 2013b).

The world of social media provides a plethora of resources for tips and advice on making these media more accessible. For example, Twitter users can be kept in the loop with current events and emerging trends in accessibility and educational technology by following certain Twitter users (e.g., @w3c_wai, @disabilitygov) or hashtag topics (e.g., #accessibility, #a11y, #edtech). Technology companies have Web pages, staff, and accounts dedicated to accessibility, such as Google's Twitter account @googleaccess and @FBaccess from the Facebook accessibility team.

Call to Action

Creamer and Creamer's (1986) model of planned change cites championship as the most important predictor of change. Student affairs professionals in all functional areas are primed to be champions for accessibility in student affairs technology and in higher education overall. Armed with theories of UD and practical knowledge of the student experience, student affairs professionals can take informed action and encourage others to do the same. Kleinglass (2005) called for leaders who are collaborative, courageous, and competent in their actions. She implored student affairs professionals to take the lead in the changing technological landscape of higher education: "Student affairs professionals must envision themselves as the leaders and experts who have the knowledge and thus power to direct the inevitable changes in the profession" (p. 35).

This call to action is not directed only at professionals in disability support services. On the contrary, the torch of accessibility must be carried by everyone in higher education. Evans, Assadi, and Herriott (2005) suggested that potential disability allies must first develop awareness of accessibility issues. Education, particularly in areas such as UD, is the next step; and skill development is the third level for developing disability allies. When student affairs professionals become confident and competent stewards of accessibility, they can encourage others to join their efforts to create change. For example, students with disabilities can be invited to serve on committees and provide feedback on their interactions with campus technologies. Resources for applying UD principles can be designed in collaboration with faculty, information technology departments, and campus facility staff. As student affairs professionals continue to embrace technology to engage students and enhance the learning environment, they must also embrace UD principles to ensure that these opportunities are accessible and welcoming to all members of the community.

Figure 4.1

GOALS Recommended Practice Indicators for Institutional Web Accessibility

- Indicator #1: Institutional Vision and Leadership Commitment
    - o Benchmark A: Commitment of administrative leadership
    - o Benchmark B: Relevant stakeholder participation

- Indicator #2: Planning and Implementation
    - o Benchmark A: Inclusion of key personnel
    - o Benchmark B: Comprehensive accessibility policy
    - o Benchmark C: Comprehensive written accessibility plan
    - o Benchmark D: Implementation of the written plan

- Indicator #3: Resources and Support
    - o Benchmark A: Focus on personnel
    - o Benchmark B: Sufficient time and effort allocated to personnel
    - o Benchmark C: Budget sufficient for institutionwide efforts
    - o Benchmark D: Training and technical support
    - o Benchmark E: Procurement, development, and use of technologies that will result in accessible Web content

- Indicator #4: Assessment
    - o Benchmark A: Evaluation of implementation progress
    - o Benchmark B: Evaluation of Web accessibility outcomes
    - o Benchmark C: Assessment results are used to improve institutional accessibility

Note. Adapted from "Introduction to the GOALS Project," by the National Center on Disability and Access to Education, retrieved from http://www.ncdae.org/goals. Copyright © 2013 by the National Center on Disability and Access to Education. Reprinted with permission.

Figure 4.2
WCAG 2.0 at a Glance

Perceivable
- Provide text alternatives for nontext content.
- Provide captions and other alternatives for multimedia.
- Create content that can be presented in different ways, including by assistive technologies, without losing meaning.
- Make it easier for users to see and hear content.

Operable
- Make all functionality available from a keyboard.
- Give users enough time to read and use content.
- Do not use content that causes seizures.
- Help users navigate and find content.

Understandable
- Make text readable and understandable.
- Make content appear and operate in predictable ways.
- Help users avoid and correct mistakes.

Robust
- Maximize compatibility with current and future user tools.

Note. Adapted from "Web Content Accessibility Guidelines (WCAG) Overview," by the World Wide Web Consortium Web Accessibility Initiative, retrieved from http://www.w3.org/WAI/intro/wcag. Copyright © 2012 by the World Wide Web Consortium. Reprinted with permission.

References

Access Technology Higher Education Network. (2012, February 29). *ATHEN report on the accessibility of Gmail and Google Calendar.* Retrieved from http://athenpro.org/google-gmail-calendar-accessibility

Americans with Disabilities Act of 1990, 42 U.S.C., § 12101 *et seq.* (2011).

Barnes, N., & Lescault, A. (2011, July). *Social media adoption soars as higher ed experiments and reevaluates its use of new communications tools.* Retrieved from http://www.umassd.edu/media/umassdartmouth/cmr/studiesandresearch/higherEd.pdf

Bordeau, D. (2011). Social media accessibility: Where are we today? *a11yBOS 2011.* Retrieved from http://www.accessibiliteweb.com/presentations/2011/a11yBOS

Boston University. (n.d.). *Campus accessibility.* Retrieved from http://www.bu.edu/disability/campus-accessibility

California State University, Office of the Chancellor. (n.d.). *Accessible technology initiative.* Retrieved from http://www.calstate.edu/accessibility

Center for Universal Design. (1997). *The principles of universal design (Version 2.0).* Raleigh, NC: North Carolina State University. Retrieved from http://www.ncsu.edu/project/design-projects/udi/center-for-universal-design/the-principles-of-universal-design

The Chronicle of Higher Education. (2012). *Almanac of higher education 2012: Technology.* Retrieved from http://chronicle.com/article/Almanac-2012-Technology/133769/?f-nav

Colorado College. (n.d.). *Campus accessibility guide.* Retrieved from http://www.coloradocollege.edu/offices/disabilityservices/campus-accessibility-guidemap

Creamer, D. G., & Creamer, E. G. (1986). Applying a model of planned change to program innovation in student affairs. *Journal of College Student Personnel, 27,* 19–26.

Evans, N., Assadi, J. L., & Herriott, T. K. (2005). Encouraging the development of disability allies. In R. Reason, E. M. Broido, T. L. Davis, & N. J. Evans (Eds.), *Developing social justice allies* (New directions for student services, No. 110, pp. 67–79). San Francisco, CA: Jossey-Bass.

Higbee, J. L., and Goff, E. (Eds.). (2008). *Pedagogy and student services for institutional transformation: Implementing universal design in higher education.* Retrieved from http://www.cehd.umn.edu/passit

Johnson, L., Adams Becker, S., Cummins, M., Estrada, V., Freeman, A., and Ludgate, H. (2013). *NMC horizon report: 2013 higher education edition.* Austin, TX: New Media Consortium.

Kleinglass, N. (2005). Who is driving the changing landscape in student affairs? In K. Kruger (Ed.), *Technology in student affairs: Supporting student learning and services* (New directions for student services, No. 112, pp. 25–38). San Francisco, CA: Jossey-Bass.

Media Access Australia. (2011). *Sociability: Social media for people with a disability.* Retrieved from http://www.mediaaccess.org.au/online-media/social-media

National Center on Disability and Access to Education. (2011). *Gaining online accessible learning through self-study (GOALS) project.* Retrieved from http://www.ncdae.org/goals

Nielsen. (2012, December). *Social media report 2012.* Retrieved from http://www.nielsen.com/us/en/reports/2012/state-of-the-media-the-social-media-report-2012.html

Pennsylvania State University. (2012). *Access ability: Accessibility and usability at Penn State.* Retrieved from http://accessibility.psu.edu

Rehabilitation Act of 1973 §504, 29 U.S.C. § 794 (2012).

Rehabilitation Act of 1973 § 508, 29 U.S.C. § 794d (2012).

Strange, C. (2000). Creating environments of ability. In H. A. Belch (Ed.), *Serving students with disabilities* (New directions for student services, No. 91, pp. 19–30). San Francisco: Jossey-Bass.

University of Alaska Anchorage. (2012). *Accessible wayfinding.* Retrieved from http://www.uaa.alaska.edu/accessibility/context/uaaefforts/accessiblespaces.cfm

University of Washington. (2013). *Disabilities, opportunities, internetworking, and technology (DO-IT).* Retrieved from http://www.washington.edu/doit

U.S. Department of Education. (1996). *Office for Civil Rights letter of finding, no. 09-95-2206.* Retrieved from http://uwctds.washington.edu/policy/09952206.RES.htm

U.S. Department of Justice. (1996). *Letter to Senator Harkin.* Retrieved from http://www.justice.gov/crt/foia/readingroom/frequent_requests/ada_tal/tal712.txt

U.S. Department of Justice. (2009a). *Letter of resolution, D.J. no. 202-51-312 Pace University.* Retrieved from http://www.ada.gov/pace_univ.htm

U.S. Department of Justice. (2009b). *Letter of resolution. DJ. no. 202-57-146 Case Western Reserve University.* Retrieved from http://www.ada.gov/case_western_univ.htm

U.S. Department of Justice. (2010a). *Settlement agreement between United States, et. al. and Arizona State University.* Retrieved from http://www.ada.gov/arizona_state_university.htm

U.S. Department of Justice. (2010b). *Letter of resolution, D.J. no. 202-48-213 Princeton University.* Retrieved from http://www.ada.gov/princeton.htm

U.S. Department of Justice. (2011). *Settlement agreement between National Federation of the Blind, et al. and Law School Admission Council.* Retrieved from http://www.ada.gov/LSAC.htm

U.S. Department of Justice. (2013). *Settlement agreement between the United States and Louisiana Tech University, no. 204-33-116.* Retrieved from http://www.ada.gov/louisiana-tech.htm

U.S. Department of Justice and U.S. Department of Education. (2010, June 29). *Joint dear colleague letter: Electronic book readers.* Retrieved from http://www2.ed.gov/about/offices/list/ocr/letters/colleague-20100629.html

WebAIM. (2013a). *University Web accessibility policies: A bridge not quite far enough.* Retrieved from http://webaim.org/articles/policies/policies_pilot

WebAIM. (2013b). *WebAIM: Web accessibility in mind.* Retrieved from http://webaim.org

Western University. (2013). *Campus maps—accessibility.* Retrieved from http://accessibility.uwo.ca/resources/maps/maps.html

World Wide Web Consortium. (2005). *Introduction to web accessibility.* Retrieved from http://www.w3.org/WAI/intro/accessibility.php

World Wide Web Consortium. (2012). *Web content accessibility guidelines (WCAG) overview.* Retrieved from http://www.w3.org/WAI/intro/wcag

Young, J. R. (2012, August 26). Campuses look to digital tools for savings, and reinvention. *The Chronicle of Higher Education.* Retrieved from http://chronicle.com/article/Campuses-Look-to-Digital/133932

Chapter 5

Technology Access
An Institutional Responsibility

Gaeir Dietrich

I n the ever-changing campus environment, student affairs professionals have the opportunity to take a leadership role in creating greater access and inclusion for all students with disabilities. With the advent of advances in technology, the need for assistance, education, and advocacy is greater than ever. At the same time, disability services offices may feel underprepared to assume this leadership role when it comes to access to technology.

Campuses may hold a lingering perception that disability services personnel are fully responsible for meeting the needs of students with disabilities, but the reality is that ensuring equal access to the learning environment requires institutionwide commitment. It requires an overarching vision that considers access to technology an integral part of the campus technology plan. Hardware, software, learning objects, online tools, websites, courseware management systems, e-books—all need to be accessible. The scope of the task can feel overwhelming, but with a determined collaborative approach, the campus can improve accessible offerings while reducing costs, improving pedagogy, and meeting the needs of all learners.

Rather than focusing on their lack of technical knowledge, student affairs personnel can continue to do what they do best: ensuring that the needs of students with disabilities are not forgotten, articulating a vision of full inclusion, and working to maintain the campus focus on meeting the needs of all students. This chapter offers background and ideas you can use on your own campus to help ensure that students with disabilities do not become casualties in the technological revolution.

Full Inclusion in the Information Age

Information and communication tools and devices, both software and hardware, are squarely at the intersection of instructional materials and civil rights. In June 2010, the U.S. Department of Justice and the U.S. Department of Education Office for Civil Rights released a *Dear Colleague* letter ("the Kindle letter") stating that any technology adopted by educational institutions must work for all students. Full inclusion for people with disabilities has long been campus policy, but the requirement for equal access to technology gives rise to unexpected and unforeseen issues.

For many years, campuses have relied on their disability services offices (DSOs) to meet the curricular access needs of students with disabilities, and the DSOs have tried to provide the auxiliary aids and services required by students for access, inclusion, and success. As long as these accommodations fell into established patterns (counseling, extra time on tests, readers, scribes, interpreters, etc.), the offices were able to fulfill students' requirements and help the campus meet its obligation under the law. However, when technology was added to the equation, the formula suddenly changed.

DSO personnel are trained in the Americans with Disabilities Act of 1990 (ADA), as amended, and Section 504 of Rehabilitation Act of 1973, as amended. They understand the needs of individual students and the obligation of the campus to provide full inclusion. Many are experts in policy, counseling, administration, education, and social work, but not necessarily in technology.

As technology has assumed a pivotal role in education, the requirements for full inclusion have taken a dramatic turn, and the DSOs have had to move from their familiar accommodation-provider role to an access-information role. The DSO has collaborated with the campus to ensure accessible infrastructure by providing information about the ADA and architectural barriers; now it must also make recommendations on how to provide accessible technology. Student affairs in general and the DSO in particular have been tasked with leading the way toward an accessible technology infrastructure on campus.

The expectation in the past was that DSO staff would remove any barriers and address any situations that interfered with full inclusion. However, with some software programs, hardware devices, and online interfaces, such accommodation is simply not possible. Short of rewriting computer code or reengineering machines, providing the same interactivity and usability to all students is not feasible. In these cases, there is no workaround, which means no equal opportunity to participate. Some technology simply cannot be accommodated, and requiring its use amounts to discrimination. The only way to ensure equal access is to evaluate usability before purchase or adoption.

Just as, in the words of former first lady Hillary Rodham Clinton (1996), it takes a village to raise a child, when it comes to full access to technology for all students, it takes a campus. As the accommodation expert on campus, the DSO can and should be part of the team, but every faculty and staff member who chooses technology, orders videos, selects books, posts to the Web, creates online courses, or creates instructional materials must participate in the process of building a more accessible infrastructure. Leadership and guidance are required at the institutional level, as all technology on campus is affected.

Access versus Accommodation

In this discussion, we are using *accommodations* to mean the solutions required by individual students to succeed and *access* to refer to the general technology infrastructure. Until recently, the focus for providing services to students with disabilities has been on accommodation. But with the sophistication of today's technology, that model is no longer practicable. We need to shift to a wider focus on general access. As we navigate this changing environment, we have to understand how access and accommodation work together, as well as the roles of both staff and faculty in the new landscape.

DSOs were originally created on campuses to help colleges and universities meet their legal obligations under the ADA and Section 504 of the Rehabilitation Act. The latter has another section, Section 508, which is worth considering in this discussion. Section 508 applies only to the federal government; it offers a template for Web accessibility and purchasing practices that, when followed, can result in greater access over time. A few states have chosen to adopt the Section 508 standards and apply them to state entities, which may or may not include state-funded colleges. Whether Section 508 applies to your particular system or not, the standards can provide a guide or metric for what access means and a model for creating a more accessible infrastructure on your campus. (For a listing of which states have adopted the Section 508 Standards, see the Georgia Tech Research Institute website at http://accessibility.gtri.gatech.edu/sitid/stateLawAtGlance.php or the Information Technology Technical Assistance and Training Center website at www.ittatc.org.)

When it comes to technology, the perspective of both the DSO and the campus administration must shift from a model of accommodation (meeting the needs of an individual student) to a model of access (adopting universal design and creating accessible infrastructure). From an inclusion perspective, creating access will promote an environment that encourages students with disabilities to be part of the mainstream—they will be naturally included in the rich, multicultural experience of campus life. From a cost-analysis perspective, access is often far less expensive than accommodation over time. It is cheaper to purchase a readymade solution than to invest in a customized one. The challenge is addressing the multifaceted campus culture while developing a strategy for the best use of limited campus resources.

In a conference presentation, Fred DiFiore—former Section 508 coordinator for the U.S. Patent and Trade Office (USPTO)—stated that in the first full year of implementing Section 508 procurement practices at USPTO, they saved more than $1 million by focusing on creating access rather than relying entirely on accommodations (Crowe & DiFiore, 2011). The better job a campus can do of purchasing, creating, and using the most accessible technology, the less it will have to spend on accommodations. Access will never fully replace the need for accommodations, but the two can work together along a continuum—a both–and solution rather than an either–or solution. Access will go only so far to meet students' needs, and additional needs will be covered by accommodations. In practice, increasing numbers of students, both with and without specific disabilities, are benefitting from the new focus on access and universal design.

The following are a few real-world strategies campuses have adopted in which access and accommodation work together to fulfill the needs of all students:

- *Greater access for students who require audio support on computers.* Install a free screen reader—such as a program that provides nonvisual desktop access (NVDA) for students who are unable to see the computer screen—on all the computers in student labs (access). Provide the more expensive dedicated software (e.g., JAWS, Window-Eyes) as needed for students who are blind and require more sophisticated features (accommodation).

- *Greater access for students who require text support to understand videos.* Purchase captioned videos or budget money for captioning in the purchase price and have the video captioned before it is used (access). Videos that are not saved or that exist in open repositories are captioned on request (accommodation).
- *Greater access for students who require audio support to understand text.* Install free text-to-speech software on all student lab computers. The software uses a computer-generated voice to read aloud any text document or text-based PDF (access). Students who need additional study support tools can request software designed specifically for individuals with learning disabilities (accommodation).
- *Greater access for all students who would like to create portable audio formats of electronic text (e-text).* Require all instructors to post only text-based PDFs; that is, no scans or pictures of text (access). Students who require a more specialized format can make that request through their DSO (accommodation).

An added bonus of adopting these strategies is that they provide access not only to students with disabilities but to all students. The examples outlined above translate into the universal design bonuses listed below.

- Captioning benefits English language learners, people with audio-processing issues, and anyone who is learning new vocabulary by allowing them to see and hear information at the same time. In addition, when captions are used online, it is possible to make the video searchable (by searching the caption text).
- Text-to-speech software can generate MP3 files. While such software is of great benefit for students with learning disabilities who need to see and hear the material at the same time, the feature is equally useful for students who commute or use portable devices and want to listen to documents on the go.
- Text-based PDFs are searchable, which is of great benefit to all students when they are studying, reviewing, or researching.

While the confluence of universal design and access makes sense to those who are familiar with both concepts, communicating the advantage of these options and obtaining full campus buy-in may take additional effort.

Creating a Shared Perspective

Which technology is or is not accessible changes rapidly over time. Some things that have never been accessible are suddenly made accessible. More alarmingly, some things that have traditionally been accessible may suddenly become inaccessible. Software changes, new devices are available, and the question of what is accessible is always in flux. Just contemplating the issue can be enough to make both nontechnical folks and mainstream computer staff want to hide in their offices. Although it is extremely helpful to both students and staff to have a campus expert on access technology, not many people have this expertise. But even without this kind of guidance, DSO staff can learn to raise accessibility issues and gather the resources for others to use in finding answers for the institution.

The first barrier to overcome is the lack of awareness about the inaccessibility of much technology. Most people assume that all campus computers, Web pages, digital files, and instructional materials are fully accessible. In fact, it is quite likely that many of them are not. Most campuses have many inaccessible resources but are blissfully unaware of this fact. Even if you do not have the expertise to make technology accessible, you can begin to educate others about what to look for.

Container Versus Content

Accessibility has two distinct facets: the container and the content. The container is the hardware or software the student needs to be able to access the content. The content consists of the documents or learning objects that are inside the container.

An accessible container will have controls that are usable by all students. It will allow text-to-speech, screen or text enlargement, keyboard navigation, and visible as well audible alerts. Accessible content will be, at the very least, text that a computer can read (i.e., not a picture of text) and videos that are captioned. Greater accessibility of documents can be created by including semantic structure (headings), text descriptions of graphics, and marking a header row on each table.

Learning management systems (LMSs) are a good example of the interplay between container and content, as the online environment is one of the most difficult for DSOs to accommodate. The LMS software (the container) must be accessible. The files, media, or learning objects (content) that the instructor uploads into the LMS must also be accessible. If the LMS shell is not accessible, even a fully accessible document uploaded into the LMS cannot be read. The student cannot get inside the container to view the content. If the LMS shell is accessible but the learning object that is loaded into the system is not accessible (a scan of a page or a video without captions), the student can open the container but not use the content inside. Both the LMS and the materials uploaded by the instructor must be accessible.

Developing or Adopting Accessible Content

If the first barrier to full inclusion is a lack of awareness, the second barrier is the perception that creating accessible content is extremely difficult and time-consuming. Although some time will be added to the content-creation phase, the amount of time involved need not be onerous. Indeed, creating materials that are accessible from the start does not necessarily add significantly to the design time, and the added planning time might even result in better overall design.

Something as simple as how links on a Web page are named can make a huge difference for access. For example, users of screen reader software can open a list of all the links that appear on a Web page. Naming those links with a fully descriptive phrase (such as "Visit the ACME Web page" as opposed to "Visit Web page") adds no extra development time but increases clarity and usability for all.

Once the content creator has learned to implement strategies for access, a huge amount of time can be saved whenever revisions are needed. For example, the simple act of using styles to create documents adds only seconds in the design phase but can save hours later by streamlining changes. Retrofitting, on the other hand, can be very time-consuming. Entering into the design phase with the idea that accessibility will be added later is a recipe for frustration. A far better strategy is to spend a little more time on planning. "Think accessible first" is becoming the catch phrase for forward-thinking campuses. In the long run, all students will benefit when materials are designed with universal access in mind.

Another significant barrier to inclusion is the adoption of inaccessible teaching tools: learning-enrichment software that does not work with assistive technology; online materials not designed for access; uncaptioned videos bundled with textbooks; e-books that are graphical (pictures of text), rather than text-based; and even open educational materials that are scans or inaccessible PDFs. Faculty and staff often assume that any digital media are automatically accessible, but digital does not equal accessible. In fact, the vast majority of these engagement options are not accessible.

If the publisher/producer of such materials has not addressed accessibility, it will be up to the institution that adopts the curriculum to find a way to ensure equal access. This brings us full circle to the fact that many disability services offices are not equipped to provide equally effective solutions for students with disabilities. Instead of dealing with this issue after the fact, faculty members and departments need to look closely at curriculum materials before they are adopted and work closely with DSOs to ensure that accommodation will be possible. If effective accommodation is not possible, instructors should find other materials.

Access and Academic Freedom

Discussions of accessibility often trigger faculty concerns about academic freedom. Academic freedom applies to the actual content that is taught in a course. In no way does the need for accessibility limit specific content, topics, or ideas. Simply said, the container, the format, and the learning object need to be accessible.

Academic freedom does not guarantee the right to do whatever one wants, only to teach the content that one wants to teach. Teachers have certain responsibilities outside selecting content, such as providing course syllabi, selecting books/course materials, teaching classes, holding office hours, participating in course reviews, and being assessed by peers.

In addition, faculty members are expected to follow state and federal laws, including laws that prohibit harassment and discrimination. Faculty members may not deny participation to members of any protected class. As "the Kindle letter" made clear, discrimination against an entire class of people by requiring technology that is not accessible to them is against the law (U.S. Department of Justice and U.S. Department of Education, 2010).

What Can Faculty Do?

Campuses need to develop a strategy that serves faculty, students, and DSO staff. While some of the barriers students face may be beyond the scope of most faculty members to address, faculty can have a direct impact on some issues, such as creating accessible documents, posting accessible learning objects, choosing accessible learning software, and teaching for all learning styles. In this way, faculty members can become partners with DSOs in creating opportunities for student success.

Although some faculty members embrace the concepts of universal design and accessibility, many believe that they do not have the time or resources to focus on issues of access. The campus can support faculty in improving access by providing clear strategies, articulating simple guidelines, and creating opportunities for professional development.

Developing a Plan

A campus can work with the DSO, the academic senate, and other stakeholders to create manageable policies regarding materials faculty members create, as well as the hardware and software that are adopted for instructional purposes.

The accessibility plans adopted by other institutions can provide a template for creating your own plan. Campuses that have developed plans in response to student complaints to the Office for Civil Rights (OCR) offer particularly strong examples to follow. While a settlement with a particular campus might not directly apply to another institution, such settlements have the advantage of having been assessed and reviewed by legal teams. The following settlements are of particular interest:

- California State University, Fullerton settlement (OCR Docket #09-03-2166)
- Pennsylvania State University settlement (OCR Docket #03-11-2020)

Among other issues, the California State University (CSU), Fullerton, settlement highlights the role that early book orders by faculty plays in ensuring that students with print disabilities are able to obtain the alternate formats for these books in a timely way. To this end, CSU Fullerton adopted a series of strategies, including requiring that information about the books being used in each course be published at the time that students register for their classes. Not only does this strategy allow DSOs time to create or obtain alternate formats for students with disabilities, it allows all students to budget for the cost of textbooks when choosing courses.

The Penn State settlement requires a wide-ranging accessibility plan that includes procurement of technology, websites, and libraries. The plan is comprehensive in approaching accessibility with training, ongoing support, and periodic assessment. The accessibility area on the Penn State website provides resources to staff and faculty to assist them in creating accessible materials (see http://accessibility.psu.edu).

Library access was also involved in a structured settlement with the University of California, Berkeley (UCB). In a widely reported 2013 agreement, UCB negotiated a landmark out-of-court settlement with

Disability Rights Advocates (DRA), a nonprofit legal group representing the rights of students with print disabilities. UCB published a comprehensive plan to improve access to course materials (DRA, 2013). The libraries are a critical part of this plan, developing a strategy to provide access to library materials for all students with print impairments.

On a broader scale, CSU's Technology Initiative provides an example of implementation at a systemwide level. In a top-down approach, the state universities developed board policy (California State University Executive Order 926) that requires all 23 campuses to conform to the Section 508 standards for procurement and Web accessibility (California State University Office of the Chancellor, 2004). The California State University website (www.calstate.edu/accessibility) offers a wealth of information and documentation.

Ideally, each institution will develop a comprehensive accessibility plan, along with detailed procedures for implementing that plan and standards of assessment for determining whether the plan is successful. The focus should be on simple, streamlined procedures that fit with your campus culture. The more such procedures can piggyback on current workflows and responsibilities, the more likely that faculty, staff, and administrators will assume the shared responsibility of ensuring inclusion for all students.

Inclusive Instruction

Curriculum development is a natural focus for creating accessibility. When accessibility is considered during the design phase, it becomes a natural part of the workflow. If you include standards for accessibility in the requirements for curriculum development, you will raise awareness and ensure that inaccessible materials are not adopted as the standard. Accessibility can also be added as part of course review, which will ensure that as technology changes, awareness about the issue of access will continue to be raised.

Strategies for accommodating students with disabilities in the classroom are consistent with universal design for learning (UDL). Many UDL strategies that benefit all students—such as using graphic organizers, presenting visual information in small chunks with plenty of white space, and building in pauses for processing and note-taking—also benefit students with disabilities. Conversely, many strategies for assisting students with disabilities can benefit all students.

Sonoma State University's EnACT (Ensuring Access Through Collaboration and Technology) project is an excellent example of how UDL can improve educational opportunities for all learners. Building on the original work of the Center for Universal Design at North Carolina State University and the Center for Applied Special Technology, the EnACT program offers simple strategies for teaching to all learning styles. The science of inclusion demonstrates that there is a nexus where pedagogy and curriculum can reduce barriers, support success, and ensure inclusion for all students (UDL-Universe, n.d.).

Professional Development

Federal and state laws give rise to campus policies. Campus policies become codified into campus procedures. Job duties are assigned, and staff members are hired to fulfill those duties and implement procedures. Unfortunately, in the absence of formal requirements to address professional development, the training that would ensure the transfer of the information and skills required to implement the policies is lacking. Even when initial training is provided, retraining is often overlooked.

A course of professional development that supports universal design and accessibility is the only way to ensure that everyone who chooses, designs, or creates learning materials is doing his or her part for access. Campuses can further support staff and faculty by developing mentoring programs to help them create accessible documents and learning objects.

Conclusion

Education in the digital age requires a new approach to ensuring equal participation on our campuses. Disability services professionals can no longer assume full responsibility for creating equal access for students. Ensuring access must be an institutional commitment, in which everyone who is involved with technology and educational materials addresses accessibility as part of the standard workflow. Only when access becomes part of mainstream thought will the needs of students with disabilities truly be served.

References

ADA Amendments Act of 2008, 42 U.S.C. § 12101 note (2011).

Americans with Disabilities Act of 1990, 42 U.S.C., § 12101 *et seq.* (2011).

California State University Office of the Chancellor. (2004, December 20). The California State University Board of Trustees policy on disability support and accommodations—Executive Order Number 926. Retrieved from http://www.calstate.edu/eo/EO-926.html

Clinton, H. R. (1996). *It takes a village.* New York, NY: Simon and Schuster.

Crowe, E., & DiFiore, F. (2011, March 17). *How to improve Section 508 e-learning compliance and workload with simple tools.* Paper presented at the 26th Annual International Technology and Persons with Disabilities (CSUN) Conference, San Diego, CA.

Disability Rights Advocates. (2013). UC Berkeley accommodations initiatives structured negotiations. Retrieved from http://www.dralegal.org/impact/cases/uc-berkeley-accommodations-initiative-structured-negotiations

Rehabilitation Act of 1973 §504, 29 U.S.C. § 794 (2012).

Rehabilitation Act of 1973 § 508, 29 U.S.C. § 794d (2012).

UDL-Universe. (n.d.). *About UDL-Universe.* Retrieved from http://enact.sonoma.edu/udl

U.S. Department of Justice and U.S. Department of Education. (2010, June 29). *Joint dear colleague letter: Electronic book readers.* Retrieved from http://www2.ed.gov/about/offices/list/ocr/letters/colleague-20100629.html

PART III

Emerging and Growing Populations and Their Impact on Higher Education

Chapter 6

Wounded Warriors

John D. Mikelson

O ver the past decade, millions of veterans have returned from serving in Iraq and Afghanistan. It is estimated that nearly 400,000 men and women returning to civilian life from recent conflicts have a service-related disability (e.g., amputation, blindness, hearing impairment) (U.S. Department of Justice, n.d.). Many more have sustained less visible injuries, such as post-traumatic stress disorder (PTSD) and traumatic brain injury (TBI), which have been called the signature injuries of these wars. Many veterans have the potential to earn postsecondary degrees and fill positions in business and industry. However, veterans and service members generally have little or no knowledge of their rights or responsibilities under the Americans with Disabilities Act of 1990 (ADA) nor have they had any experience requesting educational accommodations. In fact, coming from a military culture in which acknowledging a disability may be viewed as a form of weakness, they are unlikely to speak up about their physical or mental deficiencies.

The standards used by the military to determine disability for purposes of separation and benefits, as well as the standards used by the U.S. Department of Veterans Affairs (VA) to review disability claims, are different from the definition of disability in the ADA Amendments Act of 2008 (ADAAA) and Section 504 of the Rehabilitation Act of 1973, which are designed to improve access to accommodations for persons with disabilities in school and in the workplace. A determination by the military or the VA that a veteran did not have a disability at the completion of service does not necessarily mean that he or she does not have a disability for purposes of Section 504 or the ADA and does not necessarily limit a veteran's ability to independently document disabilities and receive academic adjustments in a postsecondary setting. Likewise, a finding by the military or the VA that a veteran is entitled to disability-related benefits or services does not mean that he or she is automatically entitled to receive academic adjustments in a postsecondary setting.

About 10% of post-9/11 vets are officially classified as disabled (Fastenberg, 2012), but the actual number is likely higher. The government sets a high bar for categorizing veterans as disabled. One out of four veterans who are "very injured" is not officially considered disabled (Heaton, Loughran, & Miller, 2012), because government regulations require the veteran to be unable to carry out day-to-day responsibilities. People with major back injuries, an inability to sleep, or psychological issues stemming from PTSD may receive no financial assistance from the federal government.

New veterans have different types of injuries than those seen in previous veterans. They primarily suffer from trauma to the head and limbs, because improvised bombs were the main weapons used against them and because body armor and improved battlefield care allowed many of them to survive wounds that in past wars would have been fatal. Women are a new group of veterans; they account for 12% of those who have sought care through the VA (*Expediting Claims,* 2013). Women have served in greater numbers in these wars than in past wars. Some female veterans are claiming PTSD owing to sexual trauma in the military, which is a new challenge from a disability rating standpoint.

Of veterans who have sought VA care:

- More than 1,600 have lost a limb; many others have lost fingers or toes.
- At least 156 are blind, and thousands of others have impaired vision.
- More than 177,000 have hearing loss, and more than 350,000 report tinnitus (noise or ringing in the ears).
- Thousands are disfigured, as many as 200 so badly that they may need face transplants. (Marchione, 2012)

Others have invisible wounds. More than 400,000 of these new veterans have been treated by the VA for a mental health problem, most commonly PTSD (Cifu, 2011). Tens of thousands have suffered TBI— mostly mild concussions from bomb blasts—and doctors do not know what is in store for them over the long term. Multiple concussions, or one soon after another, raise the risk of long-term problems. A brain injury also makes the brain more susceptible to PTSD. Many new veterans have back, shoulder, and knee problems caused or aggravated by carrying heavy packs and wearing the body armor that helped keep them alive. A recent study found that 19% required orthopedic surgery consultations and 4% needed surgery after returning from combat (Goodman et al., 2012).

Government Support for Injured and Transitioning Veterans

The U.S. Department of Defense (DoD) Office of Warrior Care Policy has the mission of ensuring that wounded, ill, injured, and transitioning service members receive high-quality care and seamless transition support through proactive leadership, responsive policy, effective oversight, and interagency collaboration (DoD, 2012). The office was established in November 2008 under the under secretary of defense for personnel and readiness. Responsibilities of the office include recovery care coordination and transition policy. Veterans may start school while they are still in recovery, before being discharged from active duty.

Disabled veterans may qualify for the Vocational Rehabilitation and Employment (VR&E) program at the Veterans Benefits Administration, authorized by Congress under Title 38 of the U.S. Code, Chapter 31, instead of the Post-9/11 GI Bill (Chapter 33), which provides financial support for education and housing to individuals with at least 90 days of aggregate military service after September 10, 2001. The Post-9/11 education benefits can be used to pay for tuition and associated fees. Approved education benefits include graduate and undergraduate degrees and vocational/technical training. The VR&E program helps veterans with service-connected disabilities prepare for, find, and keep suitable jobs. For veterans with service-connected disabilities so severe that they cannot immediately consider work, VR&E offers services to improve their ability to live as independently as possible. Educational services provided by the VR&E program include the following:

- Postsecondary training at a college, vocational, technical, or business school
- Supportive rehabilitation services, including case management, counseling, and medical referrals
- Comprehensive rehabilitation evaluation to determine abilities, skills, and interests for employment
- On-the-job training, apprenticeships, and nonpaid work experiences

After a plan is developed, a rehabilitation counselor or case manager will continue to work with the veteran to implement the plan to achieve suitable employment and/or independent living. The counselor or case manager will provide ongoing counseling, assistance, and coordination of services, such as tutorial assistance, training in job-seeking skills, medical and dental referrals, adjustment counseling, payment of training allowance, and other services required to help the veteran achieve rehabilitation.

Veterans on Campus

The post-9/11 conflicts and the Post-9/11 G.I. Bill are expected to increase the number of veterans with disabilities on our campuses, especially at 2-year institutions. Since the G.I. Bill was first introduced during World War II, millions of veterans have used their educational benefits to return to school and improve the quality of their lives. Participation in postsecondary education can play an important role in mitigating some of the effects of injury and trauma resulting from deployment into conflict areas. Learning new things and developing career goals can help veterans look to the future with hope and excitement. The average college graduate will earn nearly a million dollars more than a high school graduate over his or her lifetime (Day & Newburger, 2010). The earnings gap is even greater for persons with disabilities (National Council on Disability, 2011). Student veterans face challenges such as social adjustment, financial burdens, and reluctance to disclose disabilities. Having a disability should not deter veterans from using the educational benefits they have earned. Veterans with disabilities who are well informed about their rights under law will find that many perceived barriers and challenges can be removed or addressed, or simply do not exist.

Reasonable accommodation is a critical component of the ADA. Reasonable accommodation is any change in the educational environment or in how things are usually done that results in an equal learning opportunity. Some examples of common academic adjustments are reduced course loads, priority in class registration, extra time on examinations, real-time transcription technology or sign language interpreters for people who are deaf or hard of hearing, screen reading or magnifying software, written materials in large print or audio books for people with vision disabilities, and modified desks that will accommodate wheelchairs.

An accommodation can also mean a flexible class schedule or attendance policy to allow a student to attend VA appointments. Everyone has rights and responsibilities. In including students with disabilities in postsecondary activities, faculty members have the right to require that students demonstrate knowledge and skills essential to the course content. On the other hand, qualified students with disabilities have the right to reasonable accommodations. Neither the ADA nor Section 504 requires postsecondary schools to provide personal attendants to persons with disabilities, but many schools help students find funding for an attendant.

To receive academic adjustments, veterans with disabilities must follow college or university policies and procedures for engaging in the accommodation process. Postsecondary schools do not have a duty to find students with disabilities; rather, students must notify the school about any disability that may require academic adjustments. After admission, if academic adjustments are needed, the veteran should identify the office that provides services to students with disabilities. This is an interactive process to identify the required documentation and determine the appropriate academic adjustments. Institutions of higher education are not required to conduct or pay for an evaluation to document disability and the need for an adjustment, although some institutions do. Some institutions may help the veteran locate a qualified person to provide the required documentation. The state's vocational rehabilitation (VR) agency or a similar agency may also be a source of relevant information, through the evaluations it conducts to determine eligibility for VR services and through the Individualized Plan for Employment developed for students who are VR-eligible. Evaluations and documentation developed by military or VA personnel can be helpful in this process if they address the extent of the impairment and the need for academic adjustments. In general, documentation focusing on how the disability affects learning and other major life activities related to the postsecondary setting is appropriate. The amount of information a postsecondary school may seek from a person requesting academic adjustments is limited. The school is entitled to only the information needed to provide a sufficient basis to evaluate the student's disability and whether requested adjustments are necessary and appropriate. (For specific guidance, see Association on Higher Education and Disability, 2012.) Some postsecondary schools offer academic adjustments on a temporary basis while the veteran is collecting documentation.

The interactive process between the postsecondary institution and the student should result in academic adjustments. A school may reject a proposed academic adjustment because it would fundamentally alter the school's program (e.g., by lowering its academic standards) or because it would result in undue financial or administrative burdens. If a school decides that it cannot implement an academic adjustment, it must work with the veteran to find an effective alternative. If the academic adjustments are not meeting the veteran's needs, it is his or her responsibility to notify the school as soon as possible.

Because military culture places a high value on self-reliance, veterans who are beginning postsecondary education might find it difficult to engage in the accommodation process, even if they are eligible for services that could mitigate some of the barriers that would otherwise impede their progress. This reluctance to engage provides additional justification for the proactive removal of commonly encountered barriers at the design stage. In an institution of higher education that embraces a universal design (UD) approach, student veterans and others who experience disability are more likely to get what they need. So, too, will students who experience barriers that are not disability related, such as competing life demands. UD offers flexibility while maintaining high standards, which allows more students to get what they need and show what they know.

Campus-specific Programs and Initiatives

Colleges and universities have increased their focused support, developed programs to aid in the transition process, and streamlined resources for veterans. For example, some campuses have developed veteran-specific orientation programs to facilitate the transition of veterans into college, connect incoming veterans with veterans who are already enrolled, and connect veterans with on- and off-campus resources. These resources may include veteran-specific scholarships, access to veteran health care, and employment opportunities for veterans, family assistance, and other veteran service organizations in the area. The following are more possibilities:

- Establish partnerships with organizations that serve special populations (e.g., Latino, African American, Native American populations) to ensure that cultural issues of veterans with disabilities are addressed.
- Recruit veterans with disabilities by taking activities to veterans in hospitals, on military bases, and in local communities.
- Develop agreements between the campus disability services office and veterans rehabilitation counselors to coordinate services and provide a warm hand-off for student veterans.
- Provide outreach through online and on-site veteran networks.
- Include campus and community resources for veterans in campus orientations.
- Provide courses, presentations, and coaching for student veterans on how to talk with faculty, advocate for their own needs, deal with feelings of stigma and isolation, access assistive technology, benefit from campus services, and gain academic skills.
- Help student veterans understand the differences among the military, higher education, and the corporate world.
- Facilitate opportunities for new student veterans to be mentored online and on-site by students, faculty, or staff veterans who have been successful.
- Use the American Council on Education's Toolkit for Veteran-Friendly Institutions to share information and learn how to design and implement effective programs for veteran students (http://www.vetfriendlytoolkit.org).
- Form learning communities (cohorts) in which small groups of student veterans attend orientation and take some classes

together. Some schools have living-learning communities; others offer adaptive housing for veterans with disabilities.

- Help veterans link postsecondary education opportunities to military skill sets and map military specialties to specific academic programs. Increase the visibility and accessibility of campus and community services for veterans through peer-to-peer interactions.

Student Veterans Helping Themselves

Student veteran organizations (SVOs) support academic and social aspects of campus life and provide peer support. More than 600 SVOs across the country are affiliated with the national umbrella organization Student Veterans of America (SVA), a coalition of student veteran groups that provides assistance to help ease the transition of veterans into campus life and success. SVA's mission is "to provide military veterans with the resources, support, and advocacy needed to succeed in higher education and following graduation" (SVA, 2012, para. 1). The campus SVO may have to advocate for an on-campus veterans resource center that integrates all facets of student veteran support services, state and federal veteran programs, and student veteran organizations in one location—a gathering place that is welcoming and accessible to veterans with disabilities. The centers usually encompass work-study students and a veterans services coordinator or director. Opening a resource center may take years, but the SVO can establish a successful support network for veterans in the meantime.

Student veterans can design a website dedicated to veterans' issues and resources, and post a prominent link to the site from the college's home page. The website should include resources to support educators, service providers, employers, veterans with disabilities, and families. (For an example, see http://veterans.uiowa.edu.)

Capacity Building and Training

Institutions of higher learning may choose to create a coordinating council or task force to identify barriers for veterans with disabilities and explore ways to make campus services relevant to them. In addition to veteran-serving organizations, the group would include disability support services; recruitment and registration; and career services and tutoring centers. Such a task force would need top-down support to be sustainable. The task force is usually composed of representatives from academic and administrative departments, veterans, and members of the community. It plays a pivotal role in addressing the issues and concerns veterans face on campus and making recommendations to fix problems. The task force might also address recruitment efforts, admissions procedures, faculty understanding, outreach programs, and transfer of military credit.

A best practice for postsecondary schools is an online community of practice to improve support services for veterans and their families. Regional and national capacity-building organizations can help identify strategies for supporting transitions to education and careers for veterans with disabilities. These organizations include the veterans subgroups of the National Association of Student Personnel Administrators, the National Academic Advising Association, the Association on Higher Education and Disability, and the Disabled Student Services in Higher Education listserv.

Colleges and universities can create and distribute a brochure for faculty that covers issues relevant to veterans in postsecondary education, as well as transition guides for veteran students to local veterans centers and hospitals and to campus resources. They can also plan activities to recognize and celebrate Veterans Day, host an open house at the campus disability services office and invite local veteran-serving organizations to participate, and recognize faculty and staff who are effectively serving veterans with disabilities.

It is incumbent on postsecondary schools to provide training for faculty, teaching assistants, and staff on the positive attributes student veterans bring to campus, such as experience, motivation, and dedication;

the myths and stigmas associated with veterans with disabilities; the psychological issues many veterans experience; and the needs of student veterans. Training should include information on how traumatic brain injuries, post-traumatic stress, and other disabilities may affect these students, as well as situations that may cause problems for some veterans, such as using a laser pointer in a dark room. Schools can offer brown bag lunch programs for faculty to discuss how to work with veterans with disabilities; encourage departments to identify a faculty member (preferably a veteran) who can train, mentor, and share information and resources with others in the department; and encourage faculty to integrate curriculum and undertake research that relates to veterans with disabilities. Veterans resource centers in particular must make faculty training a priority. The goal of this training should be to make these centers obsolete.

A single training on the problems of transition or the symptoms of the signature injuries of Iraq and Afghanistan provides faculty with a very narrow and limited view of veteran students (Thompson, 2012). Institutions of higher learning need to create opportunities for faculty and staff to talk with student veterans to increase understanding of their interests and needs. Faculty members should seek out veteran resources and learn about the challenges veterans bring with them as they negotiate the transition from military service to student life.

Conclusion

When a college or university takes steps to make its veteran population visible as a distinct yet fully integrated part of the campus, it is ensuring that when funding for the veterans resource center dries up or is reallocated, the campus will remain a place that sees veterans as a member of the family. We should see these efforts not just as an obligation to repay our veterans for their service but as an opportunity to make our campuses more dynamic, more expansive, and more inclusive. Embracing veteran students is an opportunity to embrace the core function of higher education: to advance the common good.

References

ADA Amendments Act of 2008, 42 U.S.C. § 12101 note (2011).

Americans with Disabilities Act of 1990, 42 U.S.C., § 12101 *et seq.* (2011).

Association on Higher Education and Disability. (2012). *Revised guidance regarding documentation practices.* Huntersville, NC: Author.

Cifu, D. X. (2011). *Overcoming post-deployment syndrome: A six-step mission to health.* New York, NY: Demos Medical Publishing.

Day, J. C., & Newburger, E. C. (2010). *The big payoff: Educational attainment and synthetic estimates of work-life earnings.* Washington, DC: U.S. Department of Commerce, Economics and Statistics Administration.

Expediting claims or exploiting statistics? An Examination of VA's special initiative to process rating claims pending over two years. Hearing before the House Committee on Veterans' Affairs, 113th Cong. (2013, May 22) (testimony of Allison A. Hickey). Retrieved from http://veterans.house.gov/hearing/expediting-claims-or-exploiting-statistics-an-examination-of-va%E2%80%99s-special-initiative-to

Fastenberg, D. (2012, October 17). *4 challenges facing disabled veterans and how to overcome them.* Retrieved from http://jobs.aol.com/articles/2012/10/17/4-challenges-facing-disabled-veterans-and-how-to-overcome-them

Goodman, G. P., Schoenfeld, A. J., Owens, B. D., Dutton, J. R., Burks, R.,& Belmont, P. J. (2012). Non-emergent orthopaedic injuries sustained by soldiers in Operation Iraqi Freedom. *The Journal of Bone and Joint Surgery, 94*(8), 728–735. doi: 10.2106/JBJS.K.00129

Heaton, P., Loughran, D. S., & Miller, A. (2012). *Compensating wounded warriors: An analysis of injury, labor market earnings, and disability compensation among veterans of the Iraq and Afghanistan Wars.* Santa Monica, CA: RAND Corporation.

Marchione, M. (2012, May 27). *Almost half of new vets seek disability.* Retrieved from http://www.sltrib.com/sltrib/world/54192254-68/veterans-claims-percent-disability.html.csp

National Council on Disability. (2011). *National disability policy: A progress report.* October 2011. Washington DC: Author.

Post-9/11 Veterans Educational Assistance Act of 2008 (Post-9/11 G.I. Bill), 38 U.S.C., § 3301 *et seq.* (2011).

Rehabilitation Act of 1973 §504, 29 U.S.C. § 794 (2012).

Student Veterans of America. (2012). *About us.* Retrieved from http://www.studentveterans.org/about-us.html

Thompson, R. (2012, December 14). It's time to stop talking about student veterans as a deficit. *G.I. Jobs.* Retrieved from http://www.gijobs.com/blog.aspx?id=3072&blogid=143&blogid=143

U.S. Department of Defense. (2012). *Department of Defense personnel and readiness: Wounded warrior care and transition policy.* Retrieved from http://prhome.defense.gov/wwctp

U.S. Department of Justice. (n.d.). *Know your employment rights under the ADA: A guide for veterans.* Retrieved from http://adasoutheast.org/publications/ada/Employment_Rights_Under_ADA_Vets.pdf

Chapter 7

Postsecondary Education for People with Intellectual Disabilities

Tom L. Thompson

I f we examine our perceptions and expectations about the purpose of going to college, we can understand the rationale for postsecondary education for people with intellectual disabilities. Higher education prepares students for a career, provides personal enrichment, and helps them become informed citizens. These goals are important for *all* students.

Why should students with intellectual disabilities be given an opportunity to go to college? Grigal and Hart (2010) answered this way:

Most students with intellectual disabilities [ID] will not be going to college to get a degree. Many, if not most, will not have received a high school diploma. So then why would we "waste our time" giving students like this a chance to attend a college course such as art history and to participate in campus life?

The answer . . . has less to do with the courses students take and more to do with the outcomes that are possible when students with ID are afforded the opportunity to access college experiences . . . some social, some academic, and some employment. These experiences will . . . be unique for every individual who attends college. A student's experience will reflect their personal needs and goals. Some students will take many classes, while others choose to go part-time. Some students seek skills that will lead to employment; others may want to explore a new area of personal interest. . . . [C]ollege environments provide an array of experiences that most students with intellectual disabilities are not afforded during their tenure in public school: the chance to explore, define, and redefine personal goals related to adult learning, employment, and social connections. (p. 1)

Background

Postsecondary education in the United States has changed dramatically over the years—both the numbers and the diversity of students have increased significantly in the past 50 years. Students with disabilities are a newer student population, whose enrollment was significantly accelerated by the passage of the Rehabilitation Act of 1973 and the Americans with Disabilities Act of 1990 (ADA). As more of these students attend college and participate more fully in campus life, institutions are shifting from a focus on compliance, nondiscrimination, and access to a broader focus on participation, engagement, and inclusion. One student population that has not had access to many postsecondary educational opportunities is people with intellectual disabilities. Even with the support of the Individuals with Disabilities Education Act (IDEA), they face very limited opportunities after secondary education for lifelong learning, social interaction with peers, and a means to improve their employment prospects. Higher education can provide a significant milieu for young adults to acquire the habits and skills that can lead to a career and responsible citizenship (American Commonwealth Partnership, 2012).

In 2008, two momentous events occurred that gave significant impetus to broadening opportunities for all people with disabilities, including intellectual disabilities. The first was the reauthorization and amendments of the Americans with Disabilities Act (ADA Amendments Act of 2008, or ADAAA). In enacting the ADAAA, Congress recognized that "physical and mental disabilities in no way diminish a person's right to *fully participate in all aspects of society* [emphasis added], but that people with physical or mental disabilities are frequently precluded from doing so because of prejudice, antiquated attitudes, or the failure to remove societal and institutional barriers" (ADAAA § 2(a)(2)).

The second event was the passage of the Higher Education Opportunity Act, reauthorizing the Higher Education Act of 1965. The new act includes provisions and funding for the creation of a model demonstration program and coordinating center for students with intellectual disabilities. In October 2010, twenty-seven 2- and 4-year institutions or consortia of institutions received funding as comprehensive Transition and Postsecondary Programs for Students with Intellectual Disabilities (TPSIDs). The TPSID grants support programs that focus on academics and instruction, social activities, employment experiences through work-based learning and internships, and independent living. The Coordinating Center at the Institute for Community Inclusion at the University of Massachusetts Boston works with grantees to transition students with cognitive disabilities into higher education. The center is developing evaluation systems, program standards, and best practices related to the academic, social, employment, and independent living program components.

In 2013, TPSID grantees in numerous states (Florida, Ohio, North Carolina, and others) supported and facilitated the development of inclusive programs at 2-year and 4-year institutions. (For more information, see http://www.thinkcollege.net/about-us/think-college-grant-project/national-coordinating-center.)

Postsecondary Program Models

Before 2008, few postsecondary programs for students with intellectual disabilities existed in the United States; however, most community colleges and some other institutions were working with students with intellectual disabilities who had entered college through open admissions. The Association on Higher Education and Disability (AHEAD) Task Force on Students with Intellectual Disabilities in Postsecondary Education (2012) conducted a survey to assess the experience of students with intellectual disabilities enrolled in community colleges. The task force contacted approximately 30 community colleges in multiple states; 20 responded. The key findings were as follows:

- Disability services offices had years of experience in providing accommodations and guidance to students with intellectual disabilities.
- Students primarily took developmental or precollege-level courses and experimented with some college credit classes. Some colleges provided specialized offerings through continuing education.
- Students were not prepared for college courses and often performed poorly. Many parents requested additional support. Disability services sometimes referred students to other support areas on campus; for example, the tutoring center.
- Students, parents, and disability services staff were generally not satisfied with the system, which in some cases led to the creation of a program for students with intellectual disabilities.

Lewis and Clark Community College in Godfrey, Illinois, provides an example. In 1991, the school developed a life skills course for students with intellectual disabilities or autism spectrum disorders. This course expanded into a supported school-to-work program and eventually split into two programs: a College for Life continuing education program and a supported college transition program. Today Lewis and Clark is part of a national group known as the Community College Consortium on Autism and Intellectual Disabilities, formed in 2007 to facilitate advocacy and support for programs at community colleges.

Postsecondary programs for students with intellectual disabilities are developing more rapidly now, thanks to the renewed focus that came from the 2008 Higher Education Opportunity Act. Both private and public institutions are involved, and both 2-year and 4-year colleges. Most new or revamped programs focus on providing a fully inclusive experience for students, although some follow a hybrid model (partially inclusive) and some follow a segregated model (separate classes and experiences). The two primary incentives for developing a fully inclusive program are (1) research and anecdotal reports confirm that these programs provide the richest experience for both students with intellectual disabilities and other students on campus, and (2) a college must support a fully inclusive model to apply for recognition with the Department of Education as a comprehensive transition program, which enables the students at this college to apply for and receive federal financial aid to help cover program costs (tuition and fees). The following three programs illustrate investments made to sustain a program and some of the positive outcomes.

Learning Is for Everyone

The first program is a collaborative statewide effort in South Carolina that demonstrates the importance of having key advocates involved and of public-private partnerships to generate resources to launch and sustain a successful program. Donald Bailey and Caroline Bailey (2012) related this story in their book *LIFE: Learning Is for Everyone*. The College Transition

Connection (originally the Charleston Transition Connection) was a like-minded group of parents and professionals who formed a local board and ended up partnering with Think College and the National Down Syndrome Society. The group was propelled by the Bailey family's interest in creating postsecondary opportunities for their son, Donald Jr., and others like him. Donald Sr., a Charleston businessman, learned about the complexities of launching this kind of educational innovation from Susan DiFabio, a former employee of Landmark College in Vermont (a residential college for students with learning disabilities). Local people pledged financial support and raised funds; the next step was to enlist the interest and support of government representatives. Soon the mayor of Charleston was on board, along with representatives of South Carolina's special education and vocational rehabilitation communities and the director of the University of South Carolina's University Center for Excellence in Developmental Disabilities. The original board transformed into a larger task force and a steering committee.

The task force was successful in raising $300,000. It petitioned the legislature of South Carolina for an additional $300,000 to provide seed money to launch multiple programs through a request for proposals (RFP) process. The legislature approved the funds, and the local effort became a statewide initiative. The task force sent an RFP to all 70 colleges in the state, inviting them to a roundtable meeting in June 2007; 12 colleges attended. The first college to receive funding was the University of South Carolina (USC) in January 2008. Four other colleges subsequently received grants: Clemson University, Coastal Carolina University, the College of Charleston, and Winthrop University. All five colleges now have inclusive programs; the Winthrop program works closely with two local school districts.

In the Carolina LIFE program at USC, students experience college through inclusive participation in academic, social, vocational, and independent living activities. They participate in an orientation session and benefit from individual planning, academic advisement and evaluation, peer mentoring, and access to assistive technology. Carolina LIFE students create their own unique academic experiences and do not have a prescribed curriculum. The students live with other USC students in apartments near the campus.

Cutting-edge

The second program is at Edgewood College, a private Catholic university in Wisconsin. The Cutting-Edge program began as part of a doctoral research study by Dedra Hafner (2008) and was initially a noncredit pilot project. It has since become a regular college program, and 32 students have been involved since 2007. These students take undergraduate courses (three created by Cutting-Edge); reside in student housing; engage in student life events; and pursue community service, internships, and employment opportunities. Other undergraduate students with disabilities, admitted through the regular process, have also benefitted from the support available through Cutting-Edge. Non-degree Cutting-Edge students audit general education courses; those who are successful enroll in courses for credit. So far, 10 students have taken general education courses and have passed them with a grade point average of 3.0. The students have taken an average of 9.7 credits per semester.

The program surveyed undergraduate and graduate students who have contact with Cutting-Edge students; 98% said they feel comfortable attending classes, participating in campus activities, and sharing space in residence halls with students with intellectual disabilities. More than 400 students have served as peer mentors over the past 6 years—an average of 50–60 per semester. Many of these undergraduate and graduate students are recruited from college courses and gain valuable field experience; others volunteer over multiple semesters. Since leaving Edgewood College, 67% of the Cutting-Edge alumni are employed above minimum wage and 40% are continuing to pursue higher education.

Vocational Advancement and Social Skills Academy

The third program—based at Houston Community College (HCC) in Texas—is the Vocational Advancement and Skills Training (VAST) Academy. It was launched in 1990 as a small continuing education life skills transition program for 60 students. Today the VAST Academy serves more than 200 students at three locations and provides postsecondary transition programs and comprehensive support services that lead to meaningful credentials, employment, and independence. Since 1992, more than 3,000 students have participated; approximately 35% have moved successfully into college credit workforce certificate programs. HCC recently received a TPSID grant, which will be used to expand its comprehensive transition programs.

VAST offers a person-centered planning model to guide and advise students as they transition from high school to college and the workforce. Students identify a vocational degree plan, selecting from a career readiness certificate, office skills training, or a precollege pathway to prepare them for a credit workforce certificate. Freshman Success bridge courses, taught as a learning community, help provide a smooth transition from VAST to credit courses and workforce certificate programs. Students receive comprehensive support services, including advising, coaching, tutoring, mentoring, self-advocacy support, and assistance with employment. VAST works closely with disability services and has partnerships with other academic, workforce, and student service departments on campus.

VAST students actively participate in student life through the Eagles Club, student government, athletics, service-learning, and the self-advocacy group. Students who have completed their education at HCC have been hired as office assistants, filing clerks, receptionists, switchboard operators, food service workers, retail and customer service clerks, child care and teacher assistants, and landscaping attendants.

TPSID Grants

TPSIDs are federally supported 5-year grant-funded programs at institutions of higher education or consortia of institutions to create or expand high-quality, inclusive model programs for students with intellectual disabilities. Currently, 27 TPSIDs operate at 43 sites in 23 states; 14 of these sites are at community colleges. In 2013, the Think College Coordinating Center at the University of Massachusetts Boston published an annual report on TPSIDs and found the following:

- 792 students were involved in these programs by Year Two.
- 90% of students were between the ages of 18 and 28.
- 663 students enrolled in 4,806 courses (average of 7 course enrollments), with 53% in specialized courses and 47% in inclusive courses (TPSID and non-TPSID students).
- 64% of TPSID students lived with their families.
- 93% of the programs used person-centered planning; 12% of the students used academic advising and another 37% used both academic and specialized advising.
- Partnerships (187) existed between colleges and vocational rehabilitation, employers, local schools, and state departments of intellectual and developmental disabilities (IDDs).
- Funding came from institutions, vocational rehabilitation, student/family, local schools, and IDDs. Student and family fees made up 40% of the total funding.
- Certificates were the common credential; some were approved by the colleges. (Grigal, Hart, Domin, & Sulewski, 2013)

Two TPSIDs, in Florida and western New York, are described below. Both use a consortia model to enhance and expand opportunities for postsecondary education for persons with intellectual disabilities.

The Florida Consortium on Postsecondary Education and Intellectual Disabilities is based at the University of South Florida in St. Petersburg but works in partnership with the University of North Florida in Jacksonville, Lynn University in Palm Beach, and eight other Florida colleges. The consortium has three objectives: (1) expand existing transition programs at consortium campuses and fully align with criteria established for comprehensive transition programs (CTPs) for students with intellectual disabilities into higher education; (2) provide technical assistance to other postsecondary transition programs to align them with the CTP guidelines; (3) promote the development of additional postsecondary programs across Florida.

Innovative accomplishments of the consortium include the creation of a program curriculum known as Sting Ray, which has 5 domain clusters, 10 domains of learning/skills, and 115 specific competencies. This rubric guides the curriculum, and students use a Google calendar to clock contact hours for acquiring specific competencies semester by semester. The consortium has also developed a universal design for learning (UDL) online training module.

The Western New York College Consortium is based at the Institute for Innovative Transition at the University of Rochester. Three other colleges are involved: Keuka College, Monroe Community College, and Roberts Wesleyan College. There is a strong investment in each of these colleges in developing employment and work experiences for the students involved. One program is developing and using a portfolio assessment tool to track and record learning experiences. Each campus also involves students in academic courses and campus life. Susan Hetherington, principal investigator for the grant, said, "Far too few individuals with disabilities have the opportunity for competitive employment in New York. With this grant, we'll be able to work with our statewide partners to engage in systemic change and policies that will result in increased access to and support for integrated, competitive employment" (University of Rochester Medical Center, 2011, para. 3).

Disability Services Professionals as Allies

Disability services professionals are important allies who can play two significant roles in supporting students with intellectual disabilities in postsecondary education. First, the core mission of a disability services office (DSO) is to secure accommodations and access for students with disabilities, including intellectual disabilities. The interactive process for identifying needed accommodations and access is much the same for all students with disabilities; for students with intellectual disabilities, the process may include the involvement of professional staff from a program specifically structured to integrate them into the campus by focusing on academic courses, student life, and employment opportunities. Programs for students with intellectual disabilities often work closely with teaching faculty to modify the learning experience (assignments, exams, etc.), and often provide personal/academic coaching, tutoring, and mentoring.

Second, disability services professionals are campus culture "insiders" who can serve as important advisors and collaborators in establishing a program for students with intellectual disabilities. They are used to working with every area of the campus (e.g., facilities, information technology, communication systems, departmental policy/procedures), and they are always trying to ensure that the campus is increasing in accessibility. They can provide a vital link to the campus for programs for students with intellectual disabilities, which often work closely with parents, local/ state organizations, and government agencies, and whose professional staff may include people who don't understand campus culture and governance.

Another area of potential collaboration is the promotion of universal design for learning, which is strongly emphasized in the Higher Education Opportunity Act of 2008. In October 2010, the AHEAD board of directors issued a white paper about students with intellectual disabilities and campus disability services. The board expressed support for the development of inclusive programs for students with developmental and intellectual disabilities. The introduction said, in part:

Numerous programs for students with intellectual disabilities currently exist in a variety of postsecondary educational settings. While disability services professionals do not usually operate such programs, they are in a unique professional position to inform institutional decisions about designing and implementing programs that are welcoming and inclusive for students with intellectual disabilities. Where such programs already exist on a campus, disability services professionals can work with the program staff to determine how students with intellectual disabilities can access accommodations and other resources of their offices. AHEAD, in partnership with the Institute for Community Inclusion and ThinkCollege.net, will continue to provide its members with guidance on how to facilitate the full participation of students with intellectual disabilities in postsecondary educational settings. (Thompson, Weir, & Ashmore, 2011, p. 1)

AHEAD has established an ongoing task force to address issues about the inclusion of students with intellectual disabilities in postsecondary education. An excellent resource on universal design is *Universal Design in Higher Education, From Principles to Practice* (Burgstahler & Cory, 2008).

Student Affairs Professionals as Allies

Student affairs professionals in counseling, career services, residential life, student activities, and other departments are natural allies who can help develop and sustain programs for students with intellectual disabilities. Professionals in these departments are often campus leaders in diversity and social justice issues, and can help reframe campus perceptions and understanding about the experience of disability. All students go to college to discover a career path, to gain valuable insights that promote responsible citizenship, and to acquire the skills and attitudes necessary to function in society, which is increasingly global and interconnected. Student affairs professionals have always worked to advance the integration and progress of students who are marginalized (College Student Personnel Association of New York State, 2011). Staff in student affairs can create supportive and inclusive environments by reviewing their programs and services to ensure that they are incorporating the practices of universal design.

Conclusion

Professionals in higher education—especially those in disability services and student affairs, and faculty in disciplines related to the experience of disability—have an opportunity to collaborate to make the richness of college life available to an emerging population of students whose post-secondary opportunities have been severely limited in the past. It is well known that participation in higher education leads to many positive outcomes, including higher lifetime earnings and greater access to health care (Baum & Ma, 2007), but it remains to be seen how much participation in college will mean to students with intellectual disabilities.

References

ADA Amendments Act of 2008, 42 U.S.C. § 12101 note (2011).

American Commonwealth Partnership. (2012, December 26). *Final report.* Retrieved from http://www.cic.edu

Americans with Disabilities Act of 1990, 42 U.S.C., § 12101 *et seq.* (2011).

Association on Higher Education and Disability, Task Force on Students with Intellectual Disabilities in Postsecondary Education. (2012). *Survey on the experience of students with intellectual disabilities at open enrollment community colleges and other universities.* Manuscript in preparation.

Bailey, D., & Bailey, C. (2012). *LIFE: Learning is for everyone.* Bloomington, IN: iUniverse Inc.

Baum, S., & Ma, J. (2007). *Education pays.* New York, NY: The College Board.

Burgstahler, S. and Cory, R. (2008). *Universal design in higher education, from principles to practice.* Cambridge, MA: Harvard Education Publishing Group.

College Student Personnel Association of New York State. (2011). Reflecting on the past: Shaping the future of student affairs. *Journal of Student Affairs, 11*(2), 7.

Grigal, M., & Hart, D. (2010, September). *What's the point: A reflection about the purpose and outcomes of college for students with intellectual disabilities* (Insight Brief No. 2). Retrieved from http://www.thinkcollege.net/images/stories/INSIGHT_2.pdf

Grigal, M., Hart, D., Domin, F. A., & Sulewski, J. (2013). *Think College annual report.* Boston, MA: University of Massachusetts Boston, Institute for Community Inclusion.

Hafner, D. (2008). *Inclusion in postsecondary education: Phenomenological study on identifying and addressing barriers to inclusion of individuals with significant disabilities at a four-year liberal arts college.* Available from ProQuest Dissertations and Theses database. (UMI No. 3337318)

Higher Education Opportunity Act of 2008, 20 U.S.C. § 1001 note (2012).

Individuals with Disabilities Education Act, 20 U.S.C., § 1400 *et seq.* (2012).

Rehabilitation Act of 1973, 29 U.S.C. § 794 *et seq.* (2012).

Thompson, T., Weir, C., & Ashmore, J. (2011). *AHEAD white paper on students with intellectual disabilities and campus disability services.* Retrieved from http://www.ahead.org/uploads/docs/resources/Final%20SWID%20White%20Paper%20with%20PSE%20and%20DS%20Issues1.doc

University of Rochester Medical Center. (2011, October 20). *$2.35M grant to improve employment for individuals with disabilities.* Retrieved from http://www.urmc.rochester.edu/news/story/index.cfm?id=3326

Chapter 8

Fostering Success for Students with Hidden Disabilities

Lorraine E. Wolf and Jane Thierfeld Brown

S tudent affairs professionals are constantly called on to find creative ways to integrate an ever-expanding student body into an evolving set of programs and activities (El-Khawas, 2003). This endeavor often necessitates making decisions and accommodations on the fly by interpreting (and reinterpreting) policies and practices.

Students with disabilities are attending nearly every institution of higher learning. A recent report indicated that 99% of public and 100% of medium and large schools (including 2- and 4-year institutions) enroll students with disabilities (Raue & Lewis, 2011). The largest increase in the population of students with disabilities may be in the group with so-called "hidden disabilities" (Wolf, 2001). Hidden disabilities are a heterogeneous group of conditions that can compromise both academic and nonacademic functioning. Unlike physical, sensory, and mobility impairments that can be readily observed, hidden disabilities are often not immediately apparent. Although medical conditions such as irritable bowel syndrome, migraines, and closed head injury may be included in this category, the term is usually used to refer to learning disabilities, attention deficit disorder, psychiatric disorders, and autism spectrum disorders. Students with these conditions are often subject to misconceptions regarding the legitimacy of their disability. In college, they struggle in predictable ways and experience a less favorable outcome than might be expected.

Increased funding for programs, improved understanding and acceptance of the educational needs of students with disabilities, widespread education of professionals and families, and advances in diagnosis and treatment of many medical conditions have resulted in a rise in the number of high school graduates for whom college is a viable option (Wolf, 2001; Wolf & Kroesser, 2013). Earlier detection and more effective treatment of psychiatric disorders (which peak in prevalence in the college age range) mean that more students with those conditions can remain active college students (Unger, 1998). The past decade has also seen a rise in the prevalence of autism spectrum disorders and a new and capable group of students coming to campus (Wolf, Thierfeld Brown, & Bork, 2009). College students reflect roughly the same breakdown of diagnoses as students enrolled in K–12 special education: 31% learning disabilities, 18% attention disorders, and 15% psychiatric disorders (Raue & Lewis, 2011). The vast majority of students who attend college have a hidden disability.

While more successful outcomes for high school special education programs has meant that more students with disabilities enter college, the graduation rates for this population have not increased correspondingly (Barber, 2012;). Students with disabilities are less likely to complete 4-year degrees, more likely to drop out before completing any degree, and less likely to pursue graduate education. Students with disabilities made up only 8% of master's degree students and 7% of doctoral students in 2007–2008 (Planty et al., 2008). Compare that with the figure of 11% of college students in 2007–2008 reporting a disability (U.S. Department of Education, 2012) and it is clear that there is significant attrition of students with disabilities (Bell, 2011).

Challenges for Students with Hidden Disabilities

Students with hidden disabilities are most vulnerable during the first 2 years of college. They may experience significantly more difficulty making the transition from secondary to postsecondary settings than their peers without disabilities (see Wolf, 2001). They have to work harder and longer than their peers to manage the impact of their condition (Lewandowski, Codding, Kleinmann, & Tucker, 2003). Obstacles to academic success include procrastination, disorganization, poor study and time management skills, and peer pressure to socialize rather than to study (Nadeau, 1995). Many of these students have underdeveloped academic coping skills (such as self-discipline and motivation), while others are anxious and perfectionistic. Some students are overwhelmed by the dual demands of academic and residential life (Wolf, Thierfeld Brown, & Bork, 2009).

Students can struggle and fail because of the deficits associated with their individual diagnoses. For example, depression and anxiety can compromise attention as much as attention deficit disorders (see Wolf, 2001). This makes it difficult to take notes in class, study effectively, concentrate in lectures and on exams, and follow residential conduct and safety code trainings. The student with attention impairment must learn to be an excellent time manager and organizer to keep up with deadlines and demands. Students must learn to cope with difficulties in attention, self-regulation, planning and organization, memory, higher order thinking, processing speed, and thinking on their feet (such as responding when called on in class) (Denkla, 1993, 1996; Wolf & Kaplan, 2008). Many students (especially those with autism spectrum disorders and some with learning disabilities and anxiety disorders) also have low self-confidence, self-esteem, and social effectiveness (Silver, 1995). Finally, students may have achieved precollege success with the help of a strong family support network that is absent when they transition to college.

The combination of psychological, cognitive, and interpersonal difficulties often overwhelms students and their families. Many students are at risk for academic problems because they believe they can "go it alone" without asking for help or that the disability will vanish once they move into a residence hall. The desire to blend in, to be just like everyone else, is a powerful and entirely normal developmental step for youth with disabilities of any kind. However, the invisibility option is not a good strategy, as it leaves the student without much-needed supports on campus. In addition, many students with hidden disabilities are immature, crisis-driven, and motivated by outside forces rather than solid inner drives and goals (Wolf & Kaplan, 2008). They often do not realize they are in trouble until it is too late.

A perfect storm of psychological, cognitive, and interpersonal difficulties can torpedo a student's best efforts by undermining his or her use of campus resources. Support systems are critical to ensure that these students acquire the skills they need to overcome the obstacles they may face.

Self-regulation

College success demands high levels of planning, organization, and self-management in the absence of a supervising parent. These so-called "executive functions" are impaired in many conditions resulting in hidden disability (Wolf & Kaplan, 2008). Students with deficits in executive functioning usually also have deficits in academic self-regulation. They can be distinguished from their more successful peers on several key dimensions.

Successful, motivated students are characterized by the degree of self-regulation they bring to their work and their lives. For example, they understand that the use of deep strategies, such as elaborating and organizing new lecture material, is more effective than simple memorization at the last minute. These students understand how to monitor their motivation and allocation of resources (internal as well as external) to keep going when the work gets challenging. They own their learning process and know how to get back on course when they are sidetracked. These students know when and how to access support and are not afraid to ask for help when they need it. Finally, they exercise personal choice when selecting a task; they consider their goals to have worth, and they believe that the current task is important (Wolf & Kaplan, 2008).

In contrast, students who are not regulated exert less control over learning. Wolf & Kaplan (2008) termed these students "dysregulated." These students most likely depend on outside support, such as parents or peers. They are often disorganized, struggling to allocate personal resources and maintain adequate energy to follow through with tasks. They may be rigid and not be able to use feedback to change their approach, making the same bad choices and mistakes over and over. Life just happens as they struggle to manage time, materials, and space (Heilegenstein & Keeling, 1996; Wolf, 2001).

These students appear to lack the motivation to set and persist with personal goals. Goals may be imposed by others ("My father says I should study business even though I hate math") rather than motivated by the student's own desires ("I want to be a businessman—to get into a good MBA program I need to apply myself more in my math classes"). The student may have the brains and will to succeed but does not seem to know how or when to deploy them (Adelman & Vogel, 1991) and is consequently at academic risk. Dysregulation may be due to difficulties with the development and maintenance of brain systems underlying control and regulation (Wolf & Kaplan, 2008).

Student affairs professionals encounter students with regulatory problems in all areas, including residence life, student organizations, advising and counseling, career services, and student employment. The inability to follow through or sustain energy can affect social functioning to the point that the student has trouble making and maintaining positive relationships. In residence halls, the dysregulated student has a difficult time with roommate negotiations and adherence to rules and structure. Flexibility, composure, and the ability to handle conflict all affect the quality of relationships.

Students may carry their inability to regulate their emotions or follow through on tasks into student organizations and activities. Student affairs and faculty sponsors may be called on to intervene in groups in which students with hidden disabilities have acquired leadership positions but do not possess the executive function skills to carry out their roles. The student leader might require assistance in time management and organization, and the other members of the group might need some sensitivity training to learn to work with the leader. To preserve the integrity of the student group, the leader might require a high degree of supervision and support in the areas of managing budgets, assigning tasks equitably, and resolving conflict among group members.

In academics, advisors and counselors might have to provide very structured directives to help these students follow the steps involved in their curriculum and maintain a focus on graduation. Without this structure, students may haphazardly take courses and either withdraw at the last minute or fail the course. Some students have to be convinced to take required courses, which can be difficult and frustrating for the advisor. Some will take longer to complete their programs (owing to difficulties getting started and maintaining direction), necessitating extensions on housing, loans, and programs. The failure to meet academic expectations can affect financial assistance.

Substance Abuse

Alcohol and other substance abuse is not a disability, but it can exacerbate the symptoms of hidden disabilities. Nonclinical studies of undergraduate freshmen found that alcohol use and dependence are associated with significant neuropsychological deficits (Sher, Martin, Wood, & Rutledge, 1997; Zeigler et al., 2005). Alcohol abuse, especially binge drinking, impairs brain functioning involved in decision making and regulatory control (Goudriaan, Grekin, & Sher, 2007). This can further compromise development in these areas, so students who drink excessively risk poor academic outcomes by damaging the brain regions necessary for success (Goudriaan et al., 2007; Ziegler et al., 2005). College students who abuse marijuana are also at risk for ongoing cognitive deficits, including disorders of executive and attention functioning (Pope & Yurgelun-Todd, 1996; see also Wolf, Simkowitz, & Carlson, 2009). There is no evidence that college students with disabilities abuse alcohol or drugs at higher rates than their peers without disabilities (Blum, Kelly, & Ireland 2001; Miller 2013). However, it has been established that adults and adolescents with disorders of impulse control are at elevated risk for substance use and abuse (Baker, Prevatt, & Proctor, 2012; Hechtman & Weiss, 1986; Manuzza, Klein, Bessler, Malloy, & LaPadula, 1998), as are students with anxiety or mood disorders (Kushner & Sher, 1993).

Alcohol and marijuana are commonly used and abused drugs among students with attention deficit disorders; used together or alone, they can result in decreased attention and self-regulation (Baker et al., 2012). Additional diagnoses can increase this effect. For example, attention deficit disorders confer elevated risk for substance use disorders (Hechtman & Weiss, 1986; Manuzza et al., 1998), and the risk is increased if the person has other, coexisting psychiatric disorders (Hoffman et al., 1987; Murphy & Barkley 1996). A recent development on campuses is the illegal use and distribution of medications prescribed for attention disorders (Advokat, Guidry, & Martino, 2008). Dysregulated students with hidden disabilities may misuse or abuse prescribed medications, putting themselves at increased risk for the very cognitive impairment that may further undermine their chances for success on campus.

Substance abuse can exacerbate difficulties encountered by students with hidden disabilities. Every campus has programming on wellness and drug and alcohol prevention. We should pay specific attention to the unique needs of students with disabilities in these areas, yet this is rarely mentioned. We need to look at the additional stresses on students with disabilities and their outlets for this stress. Social groups, peer pressure, and bullying are additional stressors and barriers to college persistence for students with disabilities, and these are not addressed outside a counseling office. More action needs to be taken in this area.

Social Skills

Research shows that engagement and a sense of connectedness to campus are key factors in student success (Adelman & Vogel, 1991). Many hidden disabilities are accompanied by social skill deficits. Wagner, Newman, Cameto, Garza, & Levine (2005) indicated that youth with disabilities have a high prevalence of social skills deficits and are likely to participate less in structured and unstructured social activities.

Young adults with hidden disabilities may have poor social skills across a wide range of diagnoses (Rourke,1995; Wolf, 2001) and may have more problems related to social and emotional functioning than academic difficulties (Denkla, 1996; Hoy et al., 1997; Silver, 1995). These problems include talking and acting impulsively, not being able to make friends, problems making and sustaining conversation, difficulty controlling emotions and temper, and low self-confidence (see Wolf, 2001). All these problems can be amplified in the highly charged social atmosphere of a residence hall, a lecture auditorium, a sports arena, or a theater.

Poor interpersonal skills are an important reason why many students with hidden disabilities are unsuccessful at the postsecondary level (Unger, 1998; Wolf et al., 2009). The keys to maximizing academic success among students with hidden disabilities include access to university programs, availability of reasonable accommodations, and presence of appropriate support services (Wolf, 2001). Students who are successful possess personal attributes such as perseverance and self-knowledge (Barber, 2012). They develop excellent self-regulatory skills, know how to take care of themselves, and care for their brains by avoiding substances that can worsen symptoms of the disability.

Student affairs professionals can rethink ice-breaking games at orientation so as not to exclude a student with a social skills disorder (such as autism spectrum disorder) or provide written instructions for games for students with attention deficit disorder. Universal design for learning (UDL) strategies can be applied to all programming in student affairs, so that accessibility is built in to more facets of student life (Scott, McGuire, & Foley, 2003).

Technology

Text-to-speech software makes print media (including websites and other information portals) more accessible to students with learning or attention disorders. Dictation and speech-to-text software is standard in many operating systems and can be a boon to a student who struggles with writing. Graphic organizers, shared digital calendars, and planning software help dysregulated students manage their time. These tools can be seamlessly linked to class syllabi, academic calendars, and club schedules, so students are never out of touch with where they need to be and what they need to do. A wealth of social and other online media are available to assist students with social skills, connecting on and off campus, and finding resources. Most young people respond to high-tech strategies to help them deal with their difficulties, which can be a boon for students with and without disabilities.

Work Experience

Another crucial area is work skills, which take time to hone. An understanding supervisor can help ensure success on the job. Work-study and on-campus employment are very important, especially if an advisor or disability services staff member mentors the student. Job responsibilities and hours can be increased gradually. Work experience is often equally as important as a degree to the future employment success of a student.

Factors for Success

A recent study examined factors for success identified by students with disabilities (Barber, 2012). Very few students in this study sought help outside their campus; in other words, they want to be engaged on campus and not in the wider community. Parallel with this finding is the importance of having an "anchor person"—a disability services professional, advisor, or faculty member—as a mentor, to provide support and encourage persistence. The themes of connectedness to campus, involvement, and engagement with peers and faculty weave through the success stories of all students, both with and without disabilities (Johnson, 2006; Tinto, 1997).

Support is especially important at key points such as freshman year and transition to work or graduate school, where it can help students keep going when things get hard, learn to manage their expectations and their disabilities, and advocate for themselves (Izzo & Lamb, 2003). Tasks that fall naturally within the skill set of student affairs professionals are engaging students at transition points, offering campuswide outreach and training, and ensuring disability awareness.

Successful adults with learning disabilities tend to recognize, comprehend, and accept their disability (Adelman & Vogel, 1991. Self-acceptance helps students develop strong self-advocacy skills, while self-knowledge helps them set realistic goals and create effective strategies to reach them. Higher levels of self-awareness and disability awareness have been shown to correlate with improved retention rates among students with learning disabilities (see Wolf, 2001). But the very fact that students with hidden disabilities require greater self-knowledge just to access resources highlights the barriers that these students encounter in postsecondary settings.

Conclusion

Success in college and attainment of a degree lead to better long-term employment. The skills needed to succeed in college are highly transferable to employment; students who can acquire these skills and persist in college are more likely to become independent, successful adults. Student affairs professionals can help forge a path for students with hidden disabilities by increasing awareness and acceptance on campus and mentoring students and other professionals. If students with hidden disabilities are accepted and supported on campus, their future can be boundless.

References

Adelman, P., & Vogel, S. (1991). The learning disabled adult. In B. Wong (Ed.), *Learning about learning disabilities* (pp. 563–594). New York, NY: Academic Press.

Advokat, D., Guidry, D., & Martino, L. (2008). Licit and illicit use of medications for attention-deficit hyperactivity disorder in undergraduate college students. *Journal of American College Health, 56*, 601–606.

Baker, L., Prevatt, R., & Proctor, B. (2012). Drug and alcohol use in college students with and without ADHD. *Journal of Attention Disorders, 16*, 255–263.

Barber, P. (2012, September). *College students with disabilities: What factors influence successful degree completion? A case study*. Retrieved from http://www.heldrich.rutgers.edu/sites/default/files/content/College_Students_Disabilities_Report.pdf

Bell, N. (2011). Data sources: Graduate students with disabilities. *Council on Graduate Schools Communicator, 44*, 4–5.

Blum, R. W., Kelly, A., & Ireland, M. (2001). Health-risk behaviors and protective factors among adolescents with mobility impairments and learning and emotional disabilities. *Journal of Adolescent Health, 28*, 481–490.

Denkla, M. B. (1993). The child with developmental disabilities grows up: Adult residua of childhood disorders. *Neurological Clinics, 11*, 105–125.

Denkla, M. B. (1996). Biological correlates of learning and attention: What is relevant to learning disability and attention deficit hyperactivity disorder? *Journal of Developmental and Behavioral Pediatrics, 17*, 114–119.

El-Khawas, E. (2003). The many dimensions of student diversity. In S. R. Komives & D. B. Woodard (Eds.), *Student services: A handbook for the profession* (pp. 45–64). Hoboken, NJ: John Wiley and Sons.

Goudriaan, A., Grekin E., & Sher, K. (2007). Decision making and binge drinking: A longitudinal study. *Alcoholism: Clinical and Experimental Results, 31*, 928–938.

Hechtman, L., & Weiss, G. (1986). Controlled prospective 15-year follow-up of hyperactives as adults: Non-medical drug use and alcohol use and antisocial behavior. *Canadian Journal of Psychology, 31*, 557–567.

Heilegenstein, E., & Keeling, R. P. (1996). Presentation of unrecognized attention deficit disorder in college students. *Journal of American College Health, 43*, 226–228.

Hoffman, F. J., Sheldon, K. L., Minskoff, E. H., Sautter, S. W., Steidle, E. F., Baker, D. P., Bailey, M. B., & Echols, L. D. (1987). Needs of learning disabled adults. *Journal of Learning Disability, 20*, 43–52.

Hoy, C., Gregg, N., Wisenbaker, J., Manglitz, E., King, M., & Moreland, C. (1997). Depression and anxiety in two groups of adults with learning disabilities. *Learning Disability Quarterly, 20*, 280–291.

Izzo, M., & Lamb, P. (2003). Developing self-determination through career activities: Implications for rehabilitation counselors. *Journal of Vocational Rehabilitation, 19*, 71–78.

Johnson, A. L. (2006). Students with disabilities in postsecondary education: Barriers to success and implication for professionals. *VISTAS Online.* Retrieved from http://counselingoutfitters.com/Johnson.htm

Kushner, M. G., & Sher, K. J. (1993). Comorbidity of alcohol and anxiety disorders among college students: Effects of gender and family history of alcoholism. *Addictive Behaviors, 18*, 543–552.

Lewandowski, L., Codding, R., Kleinmann, A., & Tucker, K. (2003) Assessment of reading rate in postsecondary students. *Journal of Psychoeducational Assessment, 21*, 134–144.

Manuzza, S., Klein, R. G., Bessler, A., Malloy, P., & LaPadula, M. (1998). Adult psychiatric status of hyperactive boys grown up. *American Journal of Psychiatry, 155*, 493–498.

Miller, J. (2013). *Survey data recap: College students with disabilities.* Retrieved from https://docs.google.com/viewer?url=http%3A%2F%2Fwww.vcu-projectempowerment.org%2Fdocuments%2Ffacts_issue11.pdf

Murphy, K., & Barkley, R. (1996). Attention deficit disorder in adults: Comorbidities and adaptive impairments. *Comprehensive Psychiatry, 37,* 393–401.

Nadeau, K. (1995). Diagnosis and assessment of ADD in postsecondary students. *Journal on Postsecondary Education and Disability, 11*, 1–33.

Planty, M., Hussar, W., Snyder, T., Provasnik, S., Kena, G., Dinkes, R., KewalRamani, A., & Kemp, J. (2008). *The condition of education 2008 (NCES 2008-031).* Washington, DC: U.S. Department of Education, National Center for Education Statistics, Institute of Education Sciences..

Pope, H. G., & Yurgelun-Todd, D. *(*1996). The residual cognitive effects of heavy marijuana use in college students. *Journal of the American Medical Association, 275,* 521–527.

Raue, K., & Lewis, L. (2011). *Students with disabilities at degree-granting post-secondary institutions (NCES 2011-018).* Washington, DC: U.S. Department of Education, National Center for Educational Statistics.

Rourke, B. T. (Ed.). (1995). *Syndrome of nonverbal learning disabilities: Neurodevelopmental manifestations.* New York, NY: Guilford Press.

Scott, S., McGuire, J., & Foley, T. (2003). Universal design for instruction: A framework for anticipating and responding to disability and other diverse learning needs in the college classroom. *Equity and Excellence in Education, 36*(1), 40–49.

Sher, K. J., Martin, E. D., Wood, P. K., & Rutledge, P. (1997). Alcohol use disorders and neuropsychological functioning in first-year undergraduates. *Experimental and Clinical Psycholpharmacology, 5*, 304–315.

Silver, L. B. (1995). Knowledge of self: The key to self-esteem and advocacy. In Learning Disabilities Association of America (LDA) (Ed.), *Secondary education and beyond: Providing opportunities for students with learning disabilities* (pp. 223–234). Pittsburgh, PA: LDA.

Tinto, V. (1997). Classrooms as communities: Exploring the educational character of student persistence. *Journal of Higher Education, 68*, 599–623.

Unger, K. V. (1998). *Handbook on supported education: Providing services for students with psychiatric disabilities*. Baltimore, MD: PH Brooks.

U.S. Department of Education, National Center for Educational Statistics. (2012). *Digest of education statistics*. Washington, DC: Author.

Wagner, M., Newman, L., Cameto, R., Garza, N., & Levine, P. (2005). *After high school: A first look at the post-school experience of youth with disabilities*. Menlo Park, CA: SRI International.

Wolf, L. (2001). College students with ADHD and other hidden disabilities. *Annals of the NY Academy of Sciences, 931*, 385–395.

Wolf, L. E., & Kaplan, E. (2008). Executive functioning and self-regulation in young adults: Implications for neurodevelopmental learning disorders. In L. E. Wolf, H. Schreiber, & J. Wasserstein (Eds.), *Adult learning disorders: Contemporary issues* (pp. 219–246). New York, NY: Psychology Press.

Wolf, L. E., & Kroesser, S. (2013). Transition to higher education for youth with disabilities. In I. S. Baron & Rey Caserley, C. (Eds.), *Pediatric neuropsychology: Medical advances and lifespan outcomes* (pp. 344–364) London, England: Oxford University Press.

Wolf, L. E., Thierfeld Brown, J., & Bork, G. R. (2009). *Students with Asperger syndrome: A guide for college personnel*. Shawnee Mission, KS: Autism Asperger Publishing Company.

Wolf, L., Simkowitz, P., & Carlson, H. (2009). College students with attention-deficit/hyperactivity disorder. *Current Psychiatry Reports, 11*, 415–421.

Zeigler, D. W., Wang, C. C., Yoast, R. A., Dickinson, B. D., McCaffree, M. A., Robinowitz, C. B., & Sterling, M. L., Council on Scientific Affairs, American Medical Association. (2005). The neurocognitive effects of alcohol on adolescents and college students. *Preventive Medicine, 40*, 23–32.

PART IV

Examples of Best Practices

Chapter 9

Beyond the Minimum
Innovations and Partnerships

Scott N. Friedman, Eileen Connell Berger, and Kaela Parks

There are roughly 7,000 higher education institutions in the United States (U.S. Department of Education, 2012) all working to develop funds, promote student learning opportunities, and create events and programs. These institutions may have significant differences in organizational structures, pace of change, and campus culture, but as they grapple with leveraging resources and moving forward on critical issues, they would be wise to consider the work of others, including innovative models and mutually beneficial partnerships. We offer the following examples of funding and event planning approaches as an introduction to the best practices described in chapters 10 through 20.

Innovative Funding Models

Higher education must remain responsive and resilient in the face of constantly changing economic demands. Cultivating relationships and sharing resources are good ways to develop innovative strategies, but operations meant to ensure institutional compliance and program accessibility should never rely on self-support in lieu of general funds. Disability and access service areas must be funded adequately to ensure compliance. Creative funding strategies can augment core functions, but the central operation must be protected and insulated so that reasonable accommodation is never denied on the basis of cost alone. A partnership developed at Harper College is an excellent example of how core services can be complemented through partnerships that develop into robust funding streams.

Harper College: A Partnership with the Educational Foundation

Harper College is a large community college in Palatine, Illinois; among its approximately 28,000 credit students, 1,300 have a disability. The disability services office (DSO) collaborates with the school's educational foundation to secure external funding, gifts, and employee donations to support access for students with disabilities. The DSO and the foundation have worked together for more than 40 years, cultivating donor relationships that have resulted in more than $500,000 in grants and gifts, and more than $5,000,000 in state and federal grants.

To support the foundation's development efforts, the DSO provides short "cases for support" to foundation staff—one- or two-page documents that outline potential projects or areas of need for possible external funding. Foundation staff members use these documents to share information when they meet with prospective donors about opportunities to help the college.

The educational foundation has been equally successful in directing employee donations and private gifts to disability services. Through the annual Resource for Excellence campaign, many Harper College employees have donated to support six endowed scholarships for students with

128

disabilities. And private gifts helped develop an in-house captioning unit for courses and media, renovated space into a fully accessible classroom, and formally created and named the Kimball Hill Family Deaf Institute.

The DSO partners with the foundation's grants manager to identify possible opportunities, from local organizations such as Rotary Clubs and other civic groups to corporate foundations, national associations, and state and federal human services and educational agencies. The grants manager has been a vital partner in editing grant applications to ensure that narratives are tailored to funder goals and guidelines, and providing required institutional documents. The grants manager is also likely to have more direct contact with organizations, so he or she can ascertain whether DSO applications are on track for acceptance. Harper College has used corporate foundation grants to assemble a dedicated assistive technology lab and procure assistive technology resources, and has used state and federal resources to support the salaries and benefits of staff who work in the program for deaf and hard of hearing students.

A collaborative approach to strategic resource development can lead to successful partnerships with an institution's foundation. Disability services staff should bring creative and easily achievable ideas to the table so that fundraising partners can use their expertise to match ideas to the best opportunities.

Other Innovative Funding Techniques

Disability services personnel should establish connections with foundations, annual giving campaigns, and alumni offices, and pursue other creative funding techniques as well. For example, service-learning courses, regional resource sharing, and internships can all be cost-effective ways to complement core investments and move institutions forward.

With a service-learning approach, an institution can develop courses to teach students valuable skills while addressing complex challenges in a cost-effective manner (Parks, 2012). For example, computer information systems students can conduct Web accessibility reviews, multimedia design students can caption videos, geographic information systems or architecture and drafting students can generate accessible maps, and business students can research ways to use resources more effectively. The relationships are mutually beneficial: Students are learning valuable skills, and the work they complete directly benefits their community.

By developing service-learning courses, the school advances important accessibility-related initiatives with minimal use of general funds, and academic areas generate tuition while deepening connections between the students and the college or other community partners. The same kinds of mutually beneficial relationships can also be cultivated through internships and cooperative learning placements.

Institutions can also pool resources regionally to build capacity, resources, and experts. For example, with a robust alternate format material production center, it becomes possible for an institution to help defray the cost of the equipment by developing a revenue stream and completing alternate format jobs for other schools without such a center. Schools such as the University of Alaska Anchorage (2008, p. 7) and Arizona State University (T. Haven, personal communication, December 17, 2013) have offered alternate format services to others when capacity has exceeded internal demand, while schools such as Central Washington University (n.d.) provide alternate format production services for a fee through a robust center that is marketed online. For an example of a regional approach, the Alternate Text Production Center (n.d.) provides a wide range of formats, including Braille, for all 112 California community colleges as a part of standard business, at no additional cost to the participating schools, and offers a fee-for-service option for other institutions.

Other mechanisms can also be successfully leveraged to stretch dollars and bring greater accessibility to institutions; for example, offering fee-based academic coaching and learning-support programs, tapping broader diversity-related funding sources to identify disabled presenters to speak at signature events, and leveraging student technology fee dollars to not only purchase equipment but also to provide training.

The idea is not to replicate others explicitly but to consider what has worked for others, with the goal of generating local collaborations. Creative thinking can lead to novel solutions that will augment what can be accomplished with limited funding alone. Mutually beneficial relationships can help institutions reach beyond mere compliance to honor best practices and advance the profession.

Event Planning

Postsecondary institutions are required to follow the 2010 ADA Accessibility Guidelines (United States Access Board, n.d.). These are the minimum baseline standards for facility and program accessibility, but institutions can go beyond compliance to create welcoming events with programmatic access.

For example, most campuses provide basics for commencement, such as accessible seating, sign language interpreting, and ramps to the graduation platform. Some institutions choose to ensure that all aspects of commencement exceed the minimum. A disability services administrator serving on the graduation logistics committee could be tasked with selecting accessible routes and seating areas, training ushers and staff on how to assist people with disabilities, discussing access needs with students and families, and coordinating accommodations. An institution could provide extras such as multiple interpreting teams, live captioning on screens, commencement assistants for students with visual and physical disabilities, reserved seating for those with access needs, precommencement walk-throughs, accessible loading zones, increased accessible parking, and large-print signage to campus facilities.

Multicultural and diversity services offices, in concert with student affairs, can offer valuable events and programs that support, promote, and celebrate diversity, and can work together to create an environment that prepares students for the national and global diversity they will encounter in the future, both in work and in their communities (National Association of Student Personnel Administrators, 2013).

Student-led Partnerships

Partnerships led by students with disabilities and scaffolded by the disability services office can highlight the accessibility needs of a variety of students with disabilities. For example, the Harvard Graduate School of Education's student organization on International Higher Education and Disability (IHED) provides an opportunity for leadership and creation of programming as it works to ensure equal access to core activities and cocurricular expectations for achievement. Its governing structure is one of shared student leadership and flexible participation, which mitigates individual functional limitations. An advising and managing partnership with disability services creates flexibility in task structuring while students learn how best to articulate accommodation needs, and the working group provides an opportunity to develop problem solving and other professional skills. IHED students create a yearlong agenda, with one event each month and a symposium in the spring semester.

Conclusion

Whether an institution is planning large events, establishing partnerships with students, or identifying complementary funding streams, it can and should go beyond the minimum requirements to develop novel partnerships that are mutually beneficial. Doing so creates opportunities to strengthen programs and offerings, making them more inclusive and more resilient.

References

Alternate Text Production Center. (n.d). *Alternate text production center.* Retrieved from http://www.atpc.net

Central Washington University. (n.d.). *Central access.* Retrieved from http://www.cwu.edu/central-access/central-access-home

National Association of Student Personnel Administrators. (2013). *Student affairs focus areas.* Retrieved from http://www.naspa.org/focus-areas

Parks, K. (2012). *Thinking outside the box: Service learning and web accessibility.* Pre-conference session presented at the NASPA Annual Conference, Phoenix, AZ.

University of Alaska Anchorage. (2008). *University of Alaska student affairs funding request.* Retrieved from http://www.uaa.alaska.edu/studentaffairs/upload/FY09-SA-PBAC-Request.pdf

United States Access Board. (n.d.). *Guidelines and standards.* Retrieved from http://www.access-board.gov/guidelines-and-standards

U.S. Department of Education, National Center for Education Statistics. (2012). *Digest of Education Statistics, 2011* (NCES 2012-001). Retrieved from http://nces.ed.gov/fastfacts/display.asp?id=84

Chapter 10

Strengthening the Student Affairs Response Through Collaboration

Christie Gilson

T he range of disabilities that students disclose has broadened to include autism spectrum disorders, intellectual disabilities, and persistent mental health needs. Veterans from Iraq and Afghanistan who are enrolled in higher education struggle to adapt to civilian life, and their responses to traumatic brain injury and post-traumatic stress disorder can pose unique challenges to a successful student experience (Belch, 2011).

Collaboration Among Campus Units

Disabilities require support, which necessitates effective collaborations among disability services, residential life, physical and mental health providers, leadership and conduct offices, and other campus units. Student affairs professionals can take action in many areas to address the complex needs of students.

Hsieh (2010) noted that high school students who have mental health issues often benefit from more structured transitions to postsecondary education. She described a program in which incoming freshman are paired with third-year nursing students to work on building self-confidence, expanding social networks, and developing the skills necessary for academic success. Higher education institutions can offer such programs to students with psychiatric disorders through a collaboration among disability services, student counseling, and adequately supervised mental health practitioners in training. Students with all types of disabilities and chronic health conditions might benefit from transition programs (Jelfs & Richardson, 2010).

Campuses with tutoring centers might consider peer tutoring exchanges for students on the autism spectrum. Environmental changes that might seem trivial to neurotypical individuals can be vexing for students on the autism spectrum (Dente & Parkinson Coles, 2012). Students on the spectrum who are proficient in particular academic areas can tutor neurotypical students who are struggling to grasp academic concepts, while neurotypical students can reciprocate with tutoring on social situations. Coordination of such tutoring can be overseen by academic support centers, disability services, or even by the students themselves.

Peer mentoring programs organized by leadership centers, learning support offices, disability services, or academic departments can be beneficial for students with all types of disabilities (DiRamio & Spires, 2009). Such mentoring is especially powerful when the paired students share similar disabilities and can exchange success stories about navigating social situations and employment settings.

Career centers can work closely with disability services to host employment fairs designed to target students with disabilities or other diverse characteristics. Students with disabilities who lack work experience can be hired through work-study programs as interns in various student affairs offices, gaining professional experience and becoming comfortable requesting reasonable accommodations (Schaefer Enright, Conyers, & Szymanski, 1996).

Another key area for student affairs is enforcement of behavioral expectations. DiMaria (2012) suggested that conduct offices provide information to all students who use their services regarding the importance of disclosing disabilities and requesting reasonable accommodations. Solid collaboration is key to making sure that when a student discloses a disability, the response is appropriate.

Dealing Directly with Students

A basic recommendation is to hold all offices responsible for accommodating students with disabilities, rather than assuming that disability services will handle all disability-related accommodations. For example:

- When students request disability-related assistance in locating or reading online or printed publications, the requests should be fielded by library staff when possible rather than automatically handed off to disability services.
- If a student with mobility impairment requires an accessible examination table to receive health care services, the student health center should address this need.
- Disability awareness speakers and events should be coordinated by offices overseeing diversity on campus as well as by disability services.

As campus departments interact directly with students with disabilities, their staffs should be trained on disability etiquette (Lundie, 2009); appropriate threat assessment for harm to self or others (Hollingsworth,

Dunkle, & Douce, 2009); and regulations pertaining to students with disabilities, such as those of the Family Educational Rights and Privacy Act, the Health Insurance Portability and Accountability Act, the Americans with Disabilities Act of 1990, and Section 504 of the Rehabilitation Act (Simon, 2011). At the core of effective training about disability topics is the active involvement of students with disabilities.

Certainly, the disability services office and the Americans with Disabilities Act and Section 504 coordinator can be consulted. But the desired outcome should be that individual departments take responsibility for restructuring their facilities, policies, and procedures to be welcoming to all students.

References

Americans with Disabilities Act of 1990, 42 U.S.C., § 12101 *et seq*. (2011).

Belch, H. A. (2011). Understanding the experiences of students with psychiatric disabilities: A foundation for creating conditions of support and success. In M. S. Huger (Ed.), *Fostering the increased integration of students with disabilities* (New directions for student services, No. 134, pp. 73–94). San Francisco, CA: Jossey-Bass.

Dente, C. L., & Parkinson Coles, K. (2012). Ecological approaches to transition planning for students with autism and Asperger syndrome. *Children and Schools, 34,* 27–36.

DiMaria, J. T. (2012). Disciplining students with disabilities: A comparative analysis of K–12 and higher education. *Brigham Young University Education and Law Journal, 2,* 413–448.

DiRamio, D., & Spires, M. (2009). Partnering to assist disabled veterans in transition. In R. Ackerman (Ed.), *Creating a veteran-friendly campus: Strategies for transition success* (New directions for student services, No. 126, pp. 81–88). San Francisco, CA: Jossey-Bass.

Family Educational Rights and Privacy Act, 20 U.S.C., § 1232(g) (2012).

Health Insurance Portability and Accountability Act of 1996, 42 U.S.C. § 201 note (1996).

Hollingsworth, K. R., Dunkle, J. H., & Douce, L. (2009). The high-risk (disturbed and disturbing) college student. In J. H. Dunkle (Ed.), *Dealing with behavioral and psychological problems of students: A contemporary update* (New directions for student services, No. 128, pp. 37–54). San Francisco, CA: Jossey-Bass.

Hsieh, N. L. (2010). A collaboration of student nurse coaches and students with mental illnesses in a college preparation project. *Psychiatric Rehabilitation Journal, 33*(3), 200–206.

Jelfs, A., & Richardson, J. E. (2010). Perceptions of academic quality and approaches to studying among disabled and nondisabled students in distance education. *Studies in Higher Education, 35*(5), 593–607.

Lundie, D. (2009). A theory of motivation and ontological enhancement: The role of disability policy in student empowerment and institutional change. *Educational Philosophy and Theory, 41*(5), 539–552.

Rehabilitation Act of 1973 §504, 29 U.S.C. § 794 (2012).

Schaefer Enright, M., Conyers, L. M., & Szymanski, E. (1996). Career and career-related educational concerns of college students with disabilities. *Journal of Counseling and Development, 75*(2), 103–114.

Simon, J. (2011). Legal issues in serving students with disabilities in postsecondary education. In M. S. Huger (Ed.), *Fostering the increased integration of students with disabilities* (New directions for student services, No. 134, pp. 95–107). San Francisco, CA: Jossey-Bass.

Chapter 11

Universal Design in Built and Online Environments

Jamie Axelrod

C olleges and universities should consider the creation of multidisciplinary groups to guide infrastructure design on campus and create
more usable environments for diverse student populations. These
groups should include key players who have a role in designing, selecting,
and maintaining campus infrastructure; members of the campus community who understand the varying needs of individuals; staff in the disability
services office (DSO); and end users who understand and are interested in
universal or inclusive design.

Establishing and applying universal design (UD) standards in built
and online environments can greatly improve usability. Considering the
experience and needs of users before making design decisions can minimize

the need for future adaptations and retrofitting. But the institution can go further by establishing design guidelines that exceed basic compliance with the Americans with Disabilities Act of 1990 (ADA). Working with the professionals on campus who are responsible for planning and construction or programming and adopting is fundamental to this process.

An example of this collaborative approach can be seen in Northern Arizona University's Commission on Disability Access and Design (CDAD), which originated as an ADA committee but now functions as an advocate for the development of a universally designed campus. The commission includes DSO and facilities staff, the people responsible for design layout and furniture procurement, IT representatives, faculty, staff, and student end users. By strengthening ties across campus, the CDAD has been able to gain a seat at the table during the infrastructure design processes.

Universal Design in Construction

These processes have many aspects. For example, a work group might be asked to review all areas of code related to accessibility standards then apply UD principles to improve usability. Suggestions are collected in a design standards document, organized similarly to other project documents but with higher design standards. This effort demonstrates the institution's commitment to welcoming, usable, and flexible spaces. It also addresses use issues that might not be captured by the code requirements alone.

Design guidelines can be provided to professionals who are bidding to work on new construction projects or renovations on campus. Requiring bidders to address usability for all in their proposals helps those on the selection committee judge a design professional's creativity and ability to bring innovative and resourceful approaches to campus projects.

During the selection phase, questions can be incorporated that assess the goodness of fit with universal design. As a project moves into the programming/conceptual design phase, reviewers have an opportunity to explore conceptual applications of UD. As it moves into design development, experts on the commission can review the details and begin to assess the overall usability of the project. This is an excellent point in the process to confirm the application of UD to the specific project.

It is important to review construction documents and technical white papers to confirm that UD concepts have been appropriately translated into working documents for contractors and subcontractors or into the deliverables of websites, applications, and interfaces. As construction begins, commission members who had input into the UD components of the project can ensure that the appropriate designs have been incorporated.

A similar approach can be taken in creating design guidelines for furniture. The key to making sure the furniture guidelines are followed is to work with the institution's purchasing department to establish policies that ensure that furniture purchases will be reviewed for adherence.

Online Accessibility

Colleges and universities rely on technology for students to enroll in classes, receive course materials, turn in assignments, and take tests. Core technologies must be usable by all students. Reliance on technology extends to employees, who do much of their work in a digital environment; prospective students, who must submit applications online; and the public, who might visit an institution's website to look for information or to watch video clips of athletic teams. Ensuring accessibility in all these areas takes a concerted effort. Many campuses have established processes for assessing technology in relation to security and have established criteria for the levels of security a technology must demonstrate. A parallel process and criteria could be established to assess the accessibility and usability of new technologies before they are purchased. The existence of criteria for usability in technology helps purchasers understand what to look for when considering new hardware and software. Putting products through a use simulation using assistive technologies can ensure that the technology developer's claims are accurate.

Collaboration for Universal Design

Each year at Northern Arizona University, three leadership awards are presented at the Diversity and Equity Awards dinner. The CDAD honors faculty, staff, students, departments, organizations, and community members who have made outstanding contributions to the disability community. Presenting these awards and highlighting UD projects around campus nurtures the relationships that make these efforts possible and fosters ongoing collaboration.

Creating a well-designed environment takes many partners. As campus infrastructures change and evolve, all programs, from academics to transportation, must be usable by all members of the campus community. It is vital to establish and sustain working partnerships across the campus, and to provide a seat at the planning and design table for every person and group that can contribute to the creation of an inclusive campus infrastructure.

Reference

Americans with Disabilities Act of 1990, 42 U.S.C., § 12101 *et seq.* (2011).

Chapter 12

Transition to College

Jennifer L. DelRey

S arah is a first-year student at the local university. She had an Individualized Education Program (IEP) for a learning disability throughout high school, but she has not contacted the disability services office or requested any academic accommodations. As midterms approach, she is feeling overwhelmed and having difficulty keeping up with the volume of reading assignments. She has failed two quizzes and done poorly on a big exam because she ran out of time. She is scared but doesn't want to talk to anyone about it because she hated special education in high school and had been hoping to manage the university curriculum without accommodations. She knows her grades are suffering, and she is considering withdrawing from school. The instructor for her first-year experience course—a program designed to assist freshman students with the transition to college—invites the disability services coordinator to come in and lead a discussion during one of the class sessions. Sarah is surprised to learn how different the process of receiving accommodations is from what she experienced in high school. She decides to make an appointment to learn more and hopes it isn't too late to salvage her grades and complete the term successfully.

College students like Sarah may be reluctant to request the kind of accommodations they had in high school. They may think they have acquired the skills and strategies to manage postsecondary academics without accommodations, or they may want to blend in and be like their peers. However, the transition from high school to college can be difficult for students with disabilities (Madaus, 2005). It is important for these students to learn about the resources available on campus and make informed decisions.

As the number of students with disabilities entering higher education has increased, so too has the need for improved transition programs (Eckes & Ochoa, 2005). Higher education professionals must be better informed about how to assist students with disabilities in the college environment (Webster, 2004).

From IDEA to ADA

Jack's mother wants to make sure her son gets the same accommodations in college that he had in high school. During the summer before his first semester, she sends his high school IEP to the college; under the plan, Jack had unlimited time on tests, took his tests in a distraction-reduced environment, and was able to take written exams on a computer.

When classes start, Jack goes to the disability services office and is told that he needs to meet with a counselor. The counselor asks him to describe the impact of disability on his learning, but Jack has no idea how to answer. His mother always answered these types of questions. Jack's mother calls disability services and is told that she is welcome to participate in the conversation, but only if invited by her son. He is the student, and his information will not be shared without a release.

Jack and his mother make an appointment to come in together, where they learn that college students are expected to be self-advocates. Jack's high school IEP does not indicate how he was diagnosed, and while it contains a partial history of his academic struggles, the college needs an explanation of how his disability currently affects him and what accommodations might be reasonable. The counselor advises him to follow the documentation guidelines posted on the college website. Meanwhile, on the basis of the history he and his mother provide, he is offered provisional services for one semester while Jack obtains recent, updated documentation of his disability and functional limitations.

Important differences exist between K–12 processes and those at colleges and universities. Ideally, parents are educated about these differences during the high school years and can help their children transition to college; however, this does not always happen. Both high school and college personnel need to be more proactive in educating students and parents about processes and about their rights. In addition, not all students have parents working on their behalf; those who do not need support and solid information.

Many educators suggest that transition planning should begin early for students with disabilities. Students need to know the differences between the Individuals with Disabilities Education Act (IDEA), which governs K–12 education, and Section 504 of the Rehabilitation Act of 1973 and the Americans with Disabilities Act of 1990 (ADA), which govern the postsecondary environment. A lack of knowledge and understanding of their rights and responsibilities has been consistently identified as a primary factor contributing to difficulties for college students with disabilities (Webster, 2004).

Self-advocacy Skills

Self-advocacy—including being assertive, proactive, and self-determined—has been shown to increase the likelihood of success in college and beyond (Connor, 2012; Getzel & Thoma, 2008; Janiga & Costenbader, 2002).

Self-advocacy is a key component for successful transitions to adult life for students with disabilities (Reiff, 2007). But despite the documented importance of self-advocacy skills in fostering independence and success in adulthood, these skills are not usually taught in high school (Aune & Ness; 1991; Brinckerhoff, 1994; Dalke & Franzene, 1988; Ryan & Price, 1992). Many students are not directly involved in the planning of their IEPs; they find themselves responsible for advocating for their own needs for the first time when they enter college (Field, Sarver, & Shaw, 2003). Colleges should offer direct guidance to students to help them develop self-advocacy skills. In particular, students should learn about the nature of their disabilities and the available accommodations.

College personnel might consider ways to work with parents/guardians to help them with the changes they experience as their students transition to college. In particular, it might be helpful for parents (with the student's permission) to be included during the initial transition, with the goal of having the student become more skilled and independent in self-advocating.

At the College of the Holy Cross in Worcester, Massachusetts, self-advocacy is measured as a student learning outcome for all students registered with disability services. The college has found that students who experience disability have many ideas about how they can advocate for accommodations under ADA. However, the college has also found that of the learning objectives measured, self-advocacy is the area in which students need the most support and direct guidance.

Transition Programs

Focused transition programs—sometimes called bridge programs—can be an important component in facilitating the transition of students with disabilities into higher education. Integrating disability awareness into general transition activities can be beneficial, but it may not always be sufficient. Programs focused on serving students with disabilities provide a way to help these students with transitional skills and promote self-advocacy at the outset of their college careers.

Different models exist for successful bridge programs. Fairleigh Dickinson University in Hackensack, New Jersey, offers a two-week summer program for students with learning disabilities. High school seniors and graduates are exposed to college-prep skills through sessions on learning strategies, time management, computer software, and assistive technologies, as well as brainstorming, outlining, and other related topics. Landmark College in Putney, Vermont, offers a full 2-year program for postsecondary students with learning disabilities or developmental disorders.

In the National Longitudinal Study of Adolescent Health, adolescents with learning disabilities were found to be twice as likely as their peers without learning disabilities to experience emotional distress (Svetaz, Ireland, & Blum, 2000). Given the increased risk to students with learning disabilities, it is particularly important to have processes in place that promote successful transitions.

Multidisciplinary Collaboration

Transition plans and programs benefit from multidisciplinary contributions, and yet nearly 50% of collaborative efforts on college campuses are not successful, owing in part to departmental "silos" that are reinforced through institutional structures (Kezar, 2005). To increase the success rate for students with disabilities, institutions must disseminate information and promote awareness of the rights and responsibilities of students with disabilities through a learning community model. By focusing on best practices and infusing disability awareness and self-advocacy skill development throughout orientation as well as academic and cocurricular student programming, the institution can ensure that the transition from high school to college is as smooth as possible for students with disabilities, without infringing on their right to confidentiality.

References

Americans with Disabilities Act of 1990, 42 U.S.C., § 12101 *et seq.* (2011

Aune, E., & Ness, J. (1991). *Tools for transition: Preparing students with learning disabilities for post-secondary education.* Circle Pines, MN: American Guidance Services.

Brinckerhoff, L. C. (1994). Developing effective self-advocacy skills in college-bound students with learning disabilities. *Intervention in School & Clinic, 29*(4), 229.

Connor, D. J. (2012). Helping students with disabilities transition to college. *TEACHING Exceptional Children, 44*(5), 16–25.

Dalke, C. L., & Franzene, J. (1988). Secondary-postsecondary collaboration: A model of shared responsibility. *Learning Disability Focus, 4,* 38–45.

Eckes, S. E., & Ochoa, T. A. (2005). Students with disabilities: Transitioning from high school to higher education. *American Secondary Education, 33*(3), 6–20.

Field, S., Sarver, M. D., & Shaw, S. F. (2003). Self-determination: A key to success in postsecondary education for students with learning disabilities. *Remedial and Special Education, 24*(6), 339–349.

Getzel, E. E., & Thoma, C. A. (2008). Experiences of college students with disabilities and the importance of self-determination in higher education settings. *Career Development for Exceptional Individuals, 31,* 77–84.

Individuals with Disabilities Education Act, 20 U.S.C., § 1400 *et seq.* (2012).

Janiga, S. J., & Costenbader, V. (2002). The transition from high school to postsecondary education for students with learning disabilities: A survey of college service coordinators. *Journal of Learning Disabilities, 35,* 462–479.

Kezar, A. (2005). Redesigning for collaboration within higher education institutions: An exploration into the developmental processes. *Research in Higher Education, 46*(7), 831–860.

Madaus, J. W. (2005). Navigating the college transition maze: A guide for students with learning disabilities. *Teaching Exceptional Children, 37*(3), 32–37.

Rehabilitation Act of 1973 §504, 29 U.S.C. § 794 (2012).

Reiff, H. B. (2007). *Self-advocacy skills for students with learning disabilities: Making it happen in college and beyond.* New York, NY: Dude Publishing.

Ryan, A., & Price, L. (1992). Landmarks in the '90s: Addressing the needs of students with learning disabilities. *Intervention in School & Clinic, 28,* 6–20.

Svetaz, M. V., Ireland, M., & Blum, R. W. (2000). Adolescents with learning disabilities: Risk and protective factors associated with emotional well-being: Findings from the National Longitudinal Study of Adolescent Health. *Journal of Adolescent Health, 27*(5), 340–348.

Webster, D. D. (2004). Giving voice to students with disabilities who have successfully transitioned to college. *Career Development for Exceptional Individuals, 27*(2), 151–174.

Chapter 13

Experiential Education for Successful Employment Outcomes

Diane Ciarletta, Veronica L. Porter, and Marci Shaffer

According to a 2013 U.S. Bureau of Labor Statistics (BLS) report, the U.S. unemployment rate for people with disabilities in February 2012 was 13.4%, compared with 8% for those with no disability. This represents an overall increase in employment from the previous year for everyone, although the discrepancy in employment status between the two groups did not change.

Research indicates that employment outcomes improve for everyone with higher levels of education (BLS, 2013). Increasing numbers of students with disabilities are attending colleges and universities, according to a 2009 report from the U.S. Government Accountability Office (GAO). The proportion of college students with any sort of disability rose to 11% in 2008, up from 9% in 2000 (this translates to a million students nationwide). According to the GAO report, students with hidden disabilities (e.g., psychiatric or learning disabilities, autism spectrum disorder) are the fastest growing group. Students with these types of disabilities may require a different set of strategies and approaches, especially with regard to disclosure issues.

Whole-campus Approach

Higher education institutions can take advantage of their internal systems by using a whole-campus approach. This approach is working at Northeastern University in Boston, Massachusetts, through NuConnect, a wraparound experiential education model based on a strategic partnership among disability services, career services, and the cooperative education program. Professionals in these areas can be more successful in helping the students they have in common when they work together. Keeping the student's needs at the forefront, advisors create strategies that "wrap around" the student, providing support for the transition to paid work through meaningful cooperative education, internship, and postgraduate work experiences. The model is characterized by four components that have consistently led to successful outcomes: advocacy, collaboration, knowledge and resources, and feedback.

NuConnect emphasizes the counselor as both advocate and partner. It is an action-oriented model in which students are encouraged to be self-advocates. The role of the professionals is to help the student gain self-awareness, increase knowledge of the student's rights and responsibilities, and instill confidence to make choices about career paths. Disclosure is an essential part of self-advocacy. It is the counselor's job to discuss disclosure with students. Ultimately, the student will make this decision, but the counselor might encourage a student to disclose if his or her disability is severe or hidden and is related to the job. Experience has shown that students who disclose are better able to obtain accommodations and gain access to opportunities, particularly with employers who include disability as part of their diversity initiatives. When disabilities are disclosed with a well-developed strategy, the benefits outweigh the risks.

A team-based approach provides a more holistic view of the student. The team may include professionals from career services, cooperative education, and disability services, as well as academic advisors. External partners might include vocational rehabilitation professionals, agencies that work with people on the autism spectrum, and other clinicians. When appropriate, parents can be invited to be part of the team. The student is an integral part of the process and must give consent for these professionals to communicate on his or her behalf.

Disability specialists play an important role in increasing the awareness and knowledge of other partners, and counselors consult with disability specialists for advice and strategies. At Northeastern, one NuConnect strategy is to provide ongoing training for all three campus partner units. College Opportunities for Students With Disabilities offers workshops on topics such as disclosure, working with students with psychiatric and autism spectrum disorders, and student veterans with disabilities. NuConnect also uses resources and services outside the university to connect students to employment; for example, the Work Force Recruitment Program (www.wrp.gov) and the American Association for the Advancement of Science Entry Point (http://ehrweb01.aaas.org/entrypoint). Each student has a job search plan that includes a schedule with dates and action steps. Because interviewing is a critical skill, the plan includes interview practice, ideally with an employer as coach.

The fourth major component of the NuConnect model is feedback. The campus partners schedule regular meetings with students about what is and isn't working, and continually tweak the strategy. They also solicit feedback from each other.

Employer Partners

Strong relationships with employer partners are key to the success of an experiential education program. A critical strategy is to create an employer advisory committee that includes employers from various industries. The goals of the committee should include sharing best practices, increasing employment opportunities, and developing strategies to help students prepare for interviewing and success on the job. NuConnect has an employer-in-residence program through which employers meet with students for one-on-one sessions, including mock interviews, informational interviews, and résumé review. Students receive information that guides their preparation and enables them to maximize their experience. Employers provide written feedback on each student that is shared with the student and his or her advisor or counselor.

The NuConnect model has been effective in enabling students with disabilities to participate in the cooperative education program and summer internships, and to gain full-time employment. It has facilitated collaboration among professionals in career services, cooperative education, and disability services, providing them with a road map for working with students with disabilities. Shared participation in workshops and programming has also led to the development of an atmosphere of respect and understanding among the different areas, and students benefit from working with well-informed professionals in a holistic manner, using a model that is sustainable.

References

U.S. Bureau of Labor Statistics. (2013, June 12). *Persons with a disability: Labor force characteristics.* Retrieved from http://www.bls.gov/news.release/pdf/disabl.pdf

U.S. Government Accountability Office. (2009, Oct). *Higher education and disability education needs a coordinated approach to improve its assistance to schools in supporting students.* Retrieved from http://www.gao.gov/new.items/d1033.pdf

Chapter 14

Accessible Recreational and Athletic Opportunities

Matthew Springer

R ecreational opportunities for students, including those with disabilities, provide wellness, health benefits, increased independence, and an improved sense of self-esteem while promoting socialization, teamwork, and leadership skills (U.S. Government Accountability Office, 2010).

The Individuals with Disabilities Education Act (IDEA), enacted in 1975, led to an increase in the number of students with disabilities attending institutions of higher education. Postsecondary education is currently seeing an increase in the number of students of all abilities who have participated in recreational activities in the past and expect to do so in the future. In January 2013, the U.S. Department of Education Office for Civil Rights published a *Dear Colleague* letter that addressed the responsibilities of educational institutions to provide opportunities for students with disabilities to participate in recreational and extracurricular athletics. The focus of this letter is on elementary and secondary schools, but universities also must provide accessible recreation and athletic opportunities.

Facilities

Campus fitness centers are covered under the Americans with Disabilities Act of 1990, but students with disabilities still experience a lack of access. The purchase of one or two pieces of uniquely adapted equipment may serve the needs of only a few students; however, purchasing every type of adaptive equipment is cost-prohibitive and unnecessary. Universal or inclusive design is being applied to fitness equipment and recreational space, and manufacturers are including adaptive components on all equipment. Thus, rather than having segregated areas for adaptive and nonadaptive equipment, an institution can provide an integrated space with equipment that meets the needs of all users.

Meeting the needs of students with disabilities without excluding other users creates an inclusive environment. For example, a machine with adjustment levers on both sides can be used by a person who has the use of just one hand. High-contrast numbers, letters, and knobs allow use by people with low or limited vision. Weight machines that feature swing-away benches allow wheelchair users to easily move the traditional bench, lock in, and access the weights. Resistance machines that use cable-and-pulley mechanisms can be used by people with a variety of ability levels.

In a recent renovation of its recreation facilities, Wright State University in Dayton, Ohio, focused on universally accessible equipment. According to Drew Corbett, associate director for campus recreation, "We were able to select a company that manufactured fitness equipment that could be used by students both with and without a disability. These units have a low profile that allows one to see over the pieces of equipment . . . Also, adjustments for wheelchairs can be made easily" (personal communication, April 8, 2013). A supportive environment is important to students with disabilities. A workout buddy program—in which fitness center employees are paired with students with a disability to show them how to use the equipment and provide moral support—increases the students' motivation and encourages them to stay active after they graduate.

Aquatic facilities offer recreational, athletic, and therapeutic opportunities for people of all abilities. Typically, several different pools are provided to meet the goals of competition, recreation, and therapy. Competition pools—designed with deep water, large gutter systems, and water temperatures of 78–81 degrees—are suited to competition and intensive aquatic exercise, such as deep water jogging/walking/aerobics and lap swimming. Pools for recreational purposes contain current channels, or vortexes, that are valuable for resistance exercises. Warm water therapy pools offer the benefits of near-neutral buoyancy, allowing for low-impact exercise.

Accessibility varies. Direct access to the pool deck is usually limited in competition facilities, while recreational facilities may provide multiple access points. Accessibility guidelines require every pool to provide at least one alternative means of entry (a lift or sloped entry). Pools with 300 feet of wall or more must provide additional means of entry. Brian Humm, assistant director of campus recreation at the University of Akron, said, "The sloped, or zero-point, entry is preferred, as it provides the most independence to the swimmer" (personal communication, April 5, 2013).

Team Sports

Students with disabilities must have opportunities to participate in competitive and recreational athletics in activities such as wheelchair basketball, quad rugby, and other disability-specific sports. Veterans with disabilities are accustomed to intense physical recreation. As the number of these veterans increases on college and university campuses, demand for access will increase. Opening up these activities in a noncompetitive environment to *all* students gives students with disabilities a chance to include their friends who do not have mobility issues and promotes the opportunity to enhance friendships, experience teamwork, and develop mutual appreciation. However, truly competitive teams might need to be fielded in cooperation with surrounding institutions if a single school does not have a sufficient number of athletes. Providing adaptive sports doesn't necessarily mean creating a new program or facility. If a school has a basketball court it can easily provide programs for wheelchair sports; a school with a hockey rink can provide a venue for sled hockey.

It is incumbent on institutions of higher education to provide the most complete student experience possible—one that promotes student development in all areas, including athletics. A complete experience increases student success, retention, and degree completion rates. Hopefully, students with disabilities who see the benefits of recreation will want to stay active and fit, and will later seek out community fitness centers, aquatic centers, and sports teams. As Corbett noted, "The goal is independence" (personal communication, April 8, 2013).

References

Americans with Disabilities Act of 1990, 42 U.S.C., § 12101 *et seq.* (2011).

Individuals with Disabilities Education Act, 20 U.S.C., § 1400 *et seq.* (2012).

U.S. Department of Education Office for Civil Rights. (2013, January 25). *Dear colleague letter: Students with disabilities in extracurricular athletics.* Retrieved from http://www2.ed.gov/about/offices/list/ocr/letters/colleague-201301-504.pdf

U.S. Government Accountability Office. (2010, June). *Students with disabilities: More information and guidance could improve opportunity in physical education and athletics* (Report No. GAO-10-519). Retrieved from http://www.gao.gov/assets/310/305770.pdf

Additional Resources

The following organizations provide guidance in creating accessible recreation opportunities:

National Center on Accessibility (www.ncaonline.org): Supported through a cooperative agreement with the U.S. National Park Service, NCA promotes access and inclusion for people with disabilities to parks, recreation, and tourism.

National Center on Physical Activity and Disability (www.ncpad.org): NCPAD is an information center concerned with activity and disability.

National Consortium for Physical Education and Recreation for Individuals with Disabilities (www.ncperid.org): NCPERID promotes research, service delivery, and advocacy of recreation for people with disabilities.

Chapter 15

Accessible On-campus Living

Edwin A. Coolbaugh, II

Housing offices must have clear and concise procedures for disability-related accommodation requests, including request deadlines, points of contact, and room selection timelines. Housing request guidelines should be spelled out in student handbooks and applications, on housing websites, and in mailings to first-year students. Oregon State University is an example of a school whose website is well-designed, with an easy-to-navigate structure. The site gives equal weight to accessibility on the main housing and dining services pages, ensuring that the school is meeting its responsibility to provide all students with various ways to access this information.

Collaboration among housing, dining, and disability services is vital. Accommodation requests can take many forms, such as meal plan adjustments, access to private space, use of animals, and overcoming architectural barriers. The only way to ensure a good outcome is for everyone to work together.

Dining Adjustments

In the case of meal plan adjustments, the school should be able to consider various options to fulfill dietary needs and provide choices. Schools should anticipate receiving meal plan modification requests and recognize that some students will have allergies. Some schools have elected to renovate a portion of the cafeteria to create an allergy kitchen, where foods can be cooked and stored to meet specific dietary needs, reducing the chance of cross-contamination.

A student with a severe allergy might request an exemption from the meal plan requirement or a separate room for dining. It may not be possible to provide an allergen-free environment, as a contaminant could still be present in the hallways, common areas, classrooms, bathrooms, or wherever students gather. The campus should look at each case of severe allergy to determine with the student what would be the best practice in that situation and what actions the dining facilities will have to take.

Housing Accommodations

Housing offices need to establish and publicize deadlines for accommodation requests. Those deadlines should not be absolute; rather, they should be seen as a date by which a request for an accommodation has the best chance of being considered reasonable.

To understand the role of timing, consider the way the process unfolded for James, a second-year student with a diagnosis of Crohn's disease. Before his freshman year, James had provided documentation to disability services along with a request for gluten-free meals in the dining hall. The accommodation made to his meal plan was sufficient for his first year on campus, but now he is having more frequent and urgent gastrointestinal issues. His doctor has started him on regularly scheduled infusions, and just before the beginning of his second year he felt it necessary to request a single room with a private bathroom. He submitted updated documentation in support of his request, but because it was after the housing application deadline and so close to the start of the year, no rooms were available. As an accommodation, he was added to the top of the wait list. When another student ended up not needing the single room she had been assigned, he was placed in the room.

In addition to dietary needs and access to single rooms, students with disabilities might request housing-related adjustments such as roll-in showers, wider spaces for wheelchairs to maneuver, and automatic door openers or proximity readers for security systems. If possible, students with approved accommodations should be allowed to participate in the regular room selection process. This will allow them to have an experience equivalent to that of their peers while also fulfilling their specific needs. Students should be able to select rooms that already have Americans with Disabilities Act of 1990 (ADA) modifications in place or to select an unmodified room with prior understanding that the needed modifications can be made.

Allowing students to select rooms that lack updates and making incremental improvements is one way to gradually increase the number of appropriate ADA spaces in areas students find desirable. The housing liaison must be available to discuss with the student what rooms are available, or the housing office should have a list of ADA-compatible rooms by disability category. The University of Illinois at Urbana-Champaign has designed entire residence halls that are fully accessible, which earned it the 2012 Barrier-Free America award from the Paralyzed Veterans of America.

Assistance Animals

Requests for modification to the built environment typically fall under the ADA, but housing officers also must consider the Fair Housing Act (FHA), especially with regard to animals.

The 2010 revised requirements under the ADA changed the guidelines for service animals, which now include only trained dogs and miniature horses. This change affects coverage under the ADA;

it does not affect the expansive FHA definition, which requires that schools permit students to have therapy animals. The Department of Housing and Urban Development is the FHA enforcement office with regard to assistance animals.

Each college or university should have a campus policy that clarifies the distinctions among service animals, therapy animals, and pets. Animals on campus and in campus housing will continue to present a challenge, as court cases clarify the extent of the institution's responsibility in this area (Fisher, Lewis, & Schuster, 2013).

For example, a student named Michael stops by the housing office to register his cat as a service animal. The housing liaison, Sarah, tells him that the ADA identifies only trained dogs and miniature horses as service animals. She explains that the campus has a no-pet policy, except for service animals and therapy animals. Michael responds that he has an anxiety disorder and the cat allows him to remain calm. He says that having the cat with him in his room and in the classroom will enable him to be as academically successful as other students. Sarah says it sounds as though his cat is a therapy animal; to register it, he will have to provide documentation to disability services describing the nexus between his disability and the therapeutic benefit the cat provides. She adds that if the cat is approved as a therapy animal, it will be allowed in Michael's room but not in other areas of the residence hall or other buildings on campus, including classrooms. She gives Michael a copy of the campus policy on animals and contact information for the disability services office.

Housing liaisons need to work with disability services staff members to understand students' needs, and use their own expertise to identify the available options and how each option could affect the students. The presence of service or therapy animals in residence halls might give rise to concerns about other students' allergies or phobias, and the student who is using an animal will need to ensure proper health and care of the animal, keeping it clean and minimizing disruptions for others.

Secondary Barriers

Housing officers need to consider how an accommodation might affect the student's participation in social, community, and living/learning environments. Sometimes accommodations create unforeseen secondary barriers that prevent students from participating in student processes and activities.

Consider Stephanie, a freshman with muscular dystrophy who uses a power chair. Stephanie was placed in the only available accessible room, on the ground floor in an area typically populated by graduate students. She found herself cut off from the first-year activities in the upper-level freshman residence hall and unable to enjoy the social interaction she had been hoping for. Together, disability services staff and housing staff identified a creative solution: Some of the first-year activities were shifted to other locations, including the accessible lower-level lobby area and the campus center.

Student affairs professionals who work in housing and room selection should have a general understanding of how the accommodation process unfolds, but they should also work closely with the disability services office and with the students themselves to ensure quality and equality in campus living and learning opportunities.

References

Americans with Disabilities Act of 1990, 42 U.S.C., § 12101 *et seq.* (2011).

Fair Housing Act of 1968, 42 U.S.C., § 3601 *et seq.* (2011).

Fischer, W. M., Lewis, W. S., & Schuster, S. K. (2013, February). *Year in review: Legal issues update 2012 CASES.* Paper presented at the annual conference of the Association for Student Conduct Administration, St. Pete Beach, FL.

Chapter 16

Study Abroad
Inclusive Opportunities

Michele Scheib and Cerise Roth-Vinson

ollege and university mission statements often include wording on equality, nondiscrimination, and diversity, and a commitment to developing global citizens and having an international impact. However, equality and internationalization goals often do not intersect, so it can be difficult to make systemic changes that lead to inclusive international opportunities.

The main barriers to study abroad for students with disabilities are attitudinal, informational, and financial issues. There is a lack of access to information, encouragement, funding, accommodations, and role models. All these deficits can be addressed by designing study abroad programs and partnership agreements that focus on universal design and flexibility,

165

training international education staff and faculty on disability issues, and budgeting for accommodations.

Through better preparation, higher education institutions can present a diverse student body to the larger world while increasing their own retention and enriching the cultural, professional, and intellectual opportunities for a wide variety of people, including students with disabilities.

Universal Design for Study Abroad Programs

Disability social constructs and laws vary significantly around the globe—what works in the United States might be neither effective nor necessary in a different culture. To address programmatic and systemic barriers in study abroad programs, institutions can make important changes so programs are more inclusive from the beginning.

Partnership agreements between U.S. and other institutions or third-party providers should include commitments to make a program inclusive for diverse students and should set expectations for how programs can be modified if necessary. Agreements should also spell out how financial responsibilities will be shared between the parties to fund necessary accommodations for students with disabilities. The following are examples of universally beneficial program components:

- Housing options: ground floor, single occupancy, and close to public transportation.
- Referrals to English-speaking doctors, counselors, and tutors.
- Early arrival options to allow time to settle in and work out any unexpected challenges.
- Connections to local disability or diverse organizations, peers, and community groups.
- Academic options for pass/fail coursework and reduced course loads.
- Orientation materials in accessible online formats.
- Periodic consultations with students throughout the semester.

- Challenge by choice (i.e., offering activities that pose a range of challenges for all group members) and prenotification of cultural excursions and social events.
- Appropriate breaks and flexibility in scheduling.
- Availability of Internet and other communications for accessing remote support.
- Appropriate education about insurance needs and traveling with medications.
- Buildings and transportation that are accessible or modified to be accessible.
- Training for overseas faculty on disability and diverse cultures in the United States.
- Notes provided from lectures, especially those conducted in foreign languages or in experiential settings.

Another way to integrate universal design into program planning is through orientation workshops that address theoretical concepts of disability studies and other diverse identity topics, to create a context for a cohesive, interdependent, and respectful group experience abroad. All students can benefit from the development of self-advocacy and adaptability skills—they will come in handy for negotiating the unexpected abroad.

Lehigh University in Bethlehem, Pennsylvania, asks all students who are going to study abroad what organizational system they prefer, and whether they need lists or e-mail reminders. Sometimes a simple tool to stay organized helps students stay on top of details and follow through. Lehigh generalizes the supportive techniques for all students and normalizes the balance between support and personal responsibility. The orientation sessions cover disability topics the same way they do women's issues and safety abroad—these topics are useful for all students.

Inclusive Policies

U.S. higher education institutions establish policies and resources for their study abroad programs that are consistent with what they provide on their U.S. campuses, as long as they do not conflict with other countries' laws or immigration policies. This practice reduces liabilities and manages risk, and covers policies such as student codes of conduct, reporting on safety, nondiscrimination protections, and equal opportunity statements. Families of enrolled students expect the institution to train staff to recognize risks and manage emergencies, including those that are disability-related.

Equally important are health and travel insurance policies. When students go abroad, their student health plans or Medicaid or Medicare policies typically do not travel with them. To remove barriers that can prevent a student from participating and avoid crisis situations abroad, institutions should negotiate for individual or group plans that include additional benefits—such as mental health or preexisting condition coverage—at minimal cost and should make funds available to cover costs abroad (which are then repaid when the student is reimbursed by the insurance company).

Administrators of the University of California Education Abroad Program (UCEAP) know they cannot predict who will need support and who will not, so they maintain high standards in all programs for emergency planning and support. For example, they provide comprehensive insurance coverage and access to funds for upfront payment of services, such as counseling. They disseminate information about mental health and medication resources abroad, and help students prepare for conditions overseas in collaboration with counseling, health, and disability centers. While students are overseas, UCEAP continues to inform them about health, safety, and security issues, as well as available emergency travel assistance, helpful connections, and local resources. UCEAP also makes sure overseas faculty and staff know what to watch for, how to approach a student, and when to refer, and that they are trained in crisis management, incident consultation, and reporting.

Budgeting for Accommodations

Budget discussions for study abroad programs should determine how financial obligations will be handled. For example, stakeholders can create a reasonable accommodation line item, contributing a certain percentage toward an inclusion or diversity fund that all parties involved (e.g., accessibility resource centers in the United States and abroad, education abroad partners, third-party providers, scholarship providers, vocational rehabilitation offices) can access to meet accessibility and diversity commitments. While each party might have its own mechanism for accessing the funds, the contribution process is predetermined to remove questions of affordability and liability in an individual situation.

Funds might cover sign language interpreters, temporary housing if a host family placement fails, reimbursement of a portion of costs for early departure, installing ramps, personal assistance, alternative transportation arrangements, mailing or rental of assistive equipment, and upfront fees for counseling or medical care.

Dependable funding for accommodations enables staff and students to focus less on whether they can move forward when they encounter difficulties and more on how to make program components more accessible and usable by all students. For years, the Council on International Educational Exchange (CIEE) has pooled funds in its budget for participants with disabilities who require extra services or accommodations; CIEE shares expenses with the student's home institution. This arrangement makes necessary accommodations less of a crisis about a specific person and more about the rights of people with disabilities to participate.

The International Academic Programs (IAP) office at the University of Wisconsin–Madison works closely with the campus disability services office to ensure that students with disabilities have access to study abroad opportunities. The two offices work together to evaluate each situation that arises; they consider such factors as program type, location, and program duration to determine appropriate resources and relevant expenses. Depending on contributing factors, expenses are shared among participating offices and organizations; for example, program providers, consortium members, disability services, and IAP.

For decades, the nonprofit organization Mobility International USA has been a resource for finding specific answers, thinking through possible accommodation solutions, and sharing success stories to change a doubting or discouraged attitude into one that sees possibility. Its U.S. Department of State-sponsored National Clearinghouse on Disability and Exchange offers free online resources, training workshops, and referral services to increase the participation and inclusion of people with disabilities in international exchanges.

Conclusion

Students with disabilities and cultures around the world are rich in diversity, and the many potential combinations offer great possibilities for discovery and connections. It makes sense for institutions to open their study abroad programs to more inclusive programmatic, policy, and financial models. When a wide variety of students participate in these global educational programs, everyone benefits.

Chapter 17

Engaging International Students with Disabilities

Bea Awoniyi

U niversal design for learning (UDL) is defined by the Higher Education Opportunity Act of 2008 as a scientifically valid framework for guiding educational practice to engage students and support the expectation of high achievement for all students, including students with disabilities and students with limited English proficiency. Institutions of higher education that embrace the principles of universal design strive to create an inclusive community that will engage *all* students; however, international students with disabilities will still face challenges. What are some of those challenges, and what are some measures that might mitigate them?

Any student with a disability faces a number of challenges in the postsecondary environment. For a foreign national, those challenges are exacerbated by culture, language, and finance. International students have at least three different cultures with which to contend when they arrive on a college campus—they have to learn how to balance their native culture, American culture, and the culture of the college or university. Inability to manage the cultural transition may result in isolation, anxiety, and depression (Weaver, 1993). Students from societies that hold a negative view of disability may refuse to acknowledge the difficulties they are facing and may spurn assistance (Leong & Chou, 2002).

Language can be a great challenge in trying to engage international students with disabilities. Even if the students are proficient in English, they will encounter different concepts and norms as they try to understand disability supports and services. Because they are communicating in a second language, international students might either minimize or exaggerate their issues and challenges, especially mental health and family-related challenges. When students are experiencing academic challenges or social isolation, it can be especially frustrating to try to express their feelings or fully comprehend what is being asked.

Finance is another challenge international students have to contend with, especially if their support is from another country. Tuition for this group of students is very high—they pay the full cost of attendance and then some. Most do not qualify for financial aid, and very few qualify for scholarships or work-study. Language and culture can determine whether international students want to work; if they do, they are likely to be limited in both the kind of job and the number of hours they are allowed to work.

Some of these students might find it difficult to accept the idea that their academic difficulties could be the result of an undiagnosed learning disability or other acquired disability. Even if they are willing to explore the possibility of a disability, the diagnostic process can be intimidating and expensive. Many diagnosticians have limited cultural competence; they might ask questions that seem intrusive or insulting. The process might be a deterrent for international students seeking disability-related support and services, or they might not qualify because of inability to provide adequate background information. The professionals who make the diagnoses and interpret them must be sure to contextualize the histories.

To help mitigate some of these challenges, student affairs professionals should work with international/multicultural affairs and the disability services office to plan activities and programs. Collaboration among these groups should be more than just cross-referral and displaying each other's flyers; staff should get to know each other, attend activities together, and encourage their mutual students to do the same. International student organizations should include the disability office in their campus tours and welcome orientations. Student organizations and student activities can reach out to international students. Student affairs, disability services, and international and multicultural offices can plan professional development activities for themselves and for others in the campus community. As illustrated in the following two cases, professional development planners in student affairs can sponsor activities that engage and feature international students with disabilities, and use their feedback to develop future trainings.

Ishmael

Ishmael is the third of six children and the first to pursue postsecondary education outside Nigeria, his native country. He was admitted to Southern State University right after high school and could not wait to move to the United States and be independent. He arrived in August and moved into apartment-style housing on campus. In mid-November he visited the counseling center at the suggestion of one of his roommates, because he was no longer attending classes and had become withdrawn.

Ishmael completed the intake form, but it provided very little insight. In an effort to get a better understanding of Ishmael, the counselor asked questions that Ishmael considered overly personal. Ishmael was well aware that a few of his family members had mental illness, but the issue was never discussed within his family because in Nigeria mental illness is a taboo subject. Based on the personal nature of the intake interviews, Ishmael did not show up for his follow-up appointment. By the time final exams rolled around, it seemed to be too late to salvage the semester, and he was in danger of being sent back to Nigeria. Ishmael became seriously depressed. His roommates moved out, as they were not prepared to be the caretakers of another student. It was obvious that he had started to experience some form of mental illness.

Ishmael's resident assistant tried to help. He consulted with disability services, the international student center, and the counseling center. Together, they discovered that although Ishmael was on the Southern State University campus, he was not connected to it in any meaningful way. No one had tried to connect him to any small groups, because they assumed that the information was there and he could check it out on his own. The first decision was to work with Ishmael's instructors to give him time to catch up. They agreed to allow Ishmael to take his exams after the semester was over. Disability services, the international student center, and the counseling center invited two students from Nigeria to work with them—to help them understand what Ishmael was going through and to support him. Ultimately, Ishmael was able to get his academic situation under control, and he connected with the Muslim student organization, the African student organization, and other affinity groups.

This case illustrates the following points:

- Identifying the needs of foreign students is not the sole responsibility of the international office. Ishmael's roommates were the first to identify the problem, and they made appropriate suggestions about the need to engage him and encourage a sense of community. The resident assistant kept the ball rolling by facilitating collaborative efforts among the three offices. It is easy to see the value of collaborative professional development activities that encompass all areas of student interactions.
- Simply posting information about resources may not be helpful for students from different cultures. When they need it they may not know where to find it. The best practice is to create targeted

activities throughout the semester to remind students about specific resources.

- Colleges and universities offer parent orientation as a way to let parents know what resources are available to their children. However, most parents of international students cannot afford to attend orientation. Collaborative programming a few weeks into the semester, hosted by the international and multicultural offices, can help remind students about available resources.
- Cultural awareness/cultural sensitivity trainings are important; college and university professionals need to be culturally sensitive when they seek to understand and help international students.

Koino

Koino comes from a family of high achievers with high expectations. She attended one of the best schools in Taiwan but struggled with reading and comprehension through her school experience. Reading and comprehension difficulties are signs of specific learning disabilities. Koino's parents decided to send her to the United States for postsecondary education, because they believed the U.S. system of education was better suited to her. They want her to study business administration so she can return to Taiwan and manage the family business with her younger sister. Koino's immigration status requires that she be registered full time and taking at least 12 credit hours.

Within the first 2 weeks of the semester, Koino was already struggling. She could not keep up with the required reading and was having trouble comprehending the lectures because she felt the instructors talked too fast and were unclear. She went to the international student center, where staff members gave her a list of resources: library, study group sessions, instructor office hours. She met with one of her instructors, who mentioned the disability services office (DSO). DSO staff completed an intake but needed additional information about her educational experience to be able to determine that her current challenges were not the result of language or transition issues. When Koino called her parents to get the background information, they accused her of using disability services as an easy way to earn her degree.

DSO staff members told her about free read-aloud material on the Web and encouraged her to get her instructors' permission to record their lectures. The staff coached her on how to communicate her need to record and how to assure her instructors that she would use the material only for the course. Koino met with all her instructors, and they all agreed that she could use her laptop to record their lectures. She also accessed free reading tools on the Web, as well as the one her school offers to all students.

This case illustrates the following points:

- Disabilities are viewed differently in different countries. Professionals have to be willing to work with students to understand their needs and explore possible solutions with them.
- International and multicultural student offices should collaborate on programming throughout the semester. They should host multiple programs during the fall semester to remind students about available resources.
- Colleges and universities should consider a universal design approach to providing resources on campus. Some resources that DSOs provide as accommodations (e.g., reading support) can be useful for students who are second language learners.

Conclusion

The development of cultural literacy will serve student affairs professionals well. They should also make concerted efforts to engage international students and ensure that they take advantage of the services and support that will enhance their campus experience. Collaborations among student affairs, disability services, and multicultural/international student services professionals can help ensure that international students with disabilities make the most of their postsecondary experience and that institutions benefit from having these students on their campuses.

References

Higher Education Opportunity Act of 2008, 20 U.S.C. § 1001 note (2012).

Leong, F. T. L., & Chou, E. L. (2002). Counseling international students and sojourners. In P. B. Pedersen, J. G. Dragus, W. J. Lonner, & J. E. Trimble (Eds.), *Counseling across cultures* (pp. 185–207). Thousand Oaks, CA: Sage.

Weaver, G. R. (1993). Understanding and coping with cross-cultural adjustment stress. In R. M. Paige (Ed.), *Education for the intercultural experience* (pp. 137–167). Yarmouth, ME: Intercultural Press, Inc.

Chapter 18

Student Conduct and Disability

Robyn L. Hudson and Steven M. Janosik

C ollege and university administrators are faced with complex issues regarding student conduct violations, due process, and sanctioning. This is especially true when students with disabilities are involved in conduct violations that result in serious sanctions such as suspension or removal from a residence hall. Students with disabilities are a protected group and may require accommodations or other considerations in the conduct process. In this section, we provide two cases regarding student conduct and students with disabilities. We also outline best practices for handling conduct violations committed by students with disabilities in a fair and legally grounded manner, and with support and sensitivity to students who may experience difficulty navigating the student conduct process.

179

Peter

Peter is a first-year student who was overheard by his resident assistant making violent threats toward another student. After receiving sanctions from the university conduct officer, Peter writes a letter of appeal, saying that he has Asperger's syndrome, didn't understand the severity of his actions, and deserves another hearing. His appeal is denied on the basis of a court ruling that students must have established that they have a disability before the conduct process begins (*Toth v. Slippery Rock University of Pennsylvania*, 2010). Students themselves are responsible for notifying conduct officials of their disability; it is not the responsibility of other staff members at the university who may have this knowledge. The disability services office (DSO) should determine disability status. Beyond responding to requests for reasonable accommodations during hearings, conduct officers should not attempt to determine the nature, severity, or impact of a disability on behavior.

Conduct hearings are confidential; therefore, DSOs and conduct offices do not routinely share information about students. DSO staff members who know that a student with a disability is involved with student conduct can ask the student whether he or she wishes to disclose the disability. Likewise, conduct officers can refer a student who has disclosed a disability to the DSO. If the student gives informed consent, the DSO can provide assistance with accommodations during conduct proceedings, as well as advocacy and support. Once a student has disclosed a disability, reasonable accommodations must be provided during the hearing.

The same due process should be afforded to all students; this is the strongest measure an institution can take to prevent discrimination (Winik, 2005). Policies should not be changed arbitrarily or retroactively. Sensitivity to students' privacy must be maintained. Questions about mental health should be "narrowly tailored to obtain only information necessary to protect the integrity of the service to be provided and the public" (Rothstein, 1998, p. 128).

Students are not entitled to appeals or readmission hearings solely on the basis of new evidence of previously undiagnosed or undisclosed disabilities (*Carlin v. Trustees of Boston University*, 1995; *Lewin v. Medical College of Hampton Roads*, 1996). However, disability can be considered as a mitigating factor during sanctioning. Sanctions and appeal decisions should be based on the student's behavior and not on the disability per se, the student's mental health history (*Bhatt v. the University of Vermont*, 2008), or the possibility of future conduct violations related to symptoms of the disability (Rothstein, 1998).

Helen

Helen has been charged with distributing illicit drugs on campus. She has been summarily dismissed from campus until the investigation is complete and her disciplinary hearing can be scheduled. Helen claims that she is being discriminated against because she is covered under the Americans with Disabilities Act of 1990 (ADA) as a "drug addict." The student conduct officer informs her that this category is explicitly excluded from coverage under the ADA.

To be protected from discrimination, a student with a disability must be able to perform essential functions (Kaplin & Lee, 2007), including having the ability and willingness to adhere to the rules and policies of an institution (*Halpern v. Wake Forest University Health Science*, 2010). When students with disabilities are "believed to have made a threat to the safety of the campus" (Winik & Gomez, 2007, p. 413), they are subject to the same sanctions as other students. Under the ADA, misconduct owing to drug and alcohol violations is not protected (Mastiner, 2011). Violations are not excused because of medication issues, such as side effects or failure to take prescribed medications (Filo & Tee, 2004).

Best Practices

The following are best practices for student conduct officers and administrators who are dealing with students with disabilities:

- Ensure that the conduct process is the same for all students.
- Encourage students with disabilities to self-identify to the student conduct office and request accommodations for hearings. Provide a clear and simple way for students to do this.
- Request that the disability services office determine disability and recommend accommodations for students.
- Provide accommodations for hearings (e.g., sign language interpreters, scribes, braille, advocates), so students with disabilities can participate in all aspects of conduct proceedings.
- Help students with disabilities understand the conduct process and any sanctions.
- Provide resources, such as counseling or advocacy, during and after a conduct process.
- Sanction on the basis of behavior.
- Refer any student who is suspended or otherwise severely sanctioned for threatening or self-injurious behavior for a behavioral threat evaluation before final sanctioning (Rosenberg, 2010).
- Maintain thorough documentation of the entire conduct process.
- Educate and train safety officers, residence hall staff, and faculty to "anticipate and respond appropriately" to students with various types of disabilities (Shackelford, 2011, p. 3).
- Collaborate proactively with the disability services office, and consider establishing a liaison between the DSO and the conduct office.
- Develop and publish policies and procedures on conduct matters to all campus constituents in a variety of formats to ensure access (Belch & Marshak, 2006).

References

Americans with Disabilities Act of 1990, 42 U.S.C., § 12101 *et seq.* (2011).

Belch, H. A., & Marshak, L. E. (2006). Critical incidents involving students with psychiatric disabilities: The gap between state of the art and campus practice. *Journal of Student Affairs Research and Practice, 43*(3), 464–483.

Bhatt v. University of Vermont, 184 Vt. 195, 958 A.2d 637 (2008).

Carlin v. Trustees of Boston University, 907 F.Supp. 509 (D. Mass, 1995).

Filo, E., & Tee, V. (Eds.). (2004). *Disability compliance for higher education.* Horsham, PA: LRP Publications.

Halpern v. Wake Forest University Health Science, 268 F.R.D. 264 (M.D. N.C. 2010).

Kaplin, W. A., & Lee, B. A. (2007). *The law of higher education* (4th ed.). San Francisco, CA: Jossey-Bass.

Lewin v. Medical College of Hampton Roads, 910 F.Supp 1161, 1116 (E.D. Va, 1996).

Mastiner, M. R. (2011). Medical marijuana accommodations not necessary. *Disability Compliance for Higher Education, 16*(12), 3.

Rosenberg, R. (2010). Perform threat assessment before dismissing students with psychiatric disabilities. *Disability Compliance for Higher Education 15*(8), 4.

Rothstein, L. F. (1998). Higher education and disabilities: Trends and developments. *Stetson Law Review, 125,* 119–140.

Shackelford, A. L. (2011). Ensure those who deal with conduct issues understand challenges of working with students with disabilities. *Disability Compliance for Higher Education, 16*(7), 3.

Toth v. Slippery Rock University of Pennsylvania, Pa. Comm. 6 A.3d 1082 (2010).

Winik, S. (Ed.). (2005). *Disability compliance for higher education 2005 yearbook.* Horsham, PA: LRP Publications.

Winik, S. L., & Gomez, C. (Eds.). (2007). *Disability compliance for higher education 2007 yearbook.* Horsham, PA: LRP Publications.

Chapter 19

Intersectionality
Identity Re-formation

Karen Bishop Morris and Jacquelyn Bustos

L ike other units that interface with students from diverse backgrounds, the university writing program plays a significant role in preparing students for success. English composition is a unique discipline in that writing pedagogy is focused on (a) teaching reflective practice to faculty and students, and (b) constructing meaning out of multiplicity. Composition skills are crucial throughout the general education curriculum. Orienting students to the academy and enhancing critical thinking skills are priorities for all students, but especially for those from marginalized backgrounds as defined by race, class, gender, sexuality, or disability.

How do we create learning environments throughout the core curriculum that allow students to confront and critique their various identities? What opportunities exist to reveal and maximize the "inextricable nature of an individual's various identities at both individual and societal levels" (Sims, 2013, p. 6)? What should our collective approach be for students who do not self-identify as disabled to the disability services office? For example, wounded warriors who often reveal and reflect upon their disability in general education courses? Helping students negotiate a new context—the university—is about teaching them to assert control over their multifaceted identities. In *Black Sexual Politics*, Collins (2005) wrote, "Intersectional paradigms view race, class, gender, sexuality, ethnicity, and age, among others, as mutually constructing systems of power. Because these systems permeate all social relations, untangling their effects in any given situation or for any given population remains difficult" (p. 11). The confluence of these multiple identities can present huge risks for students, staff, and administrators but also a huge reward if we develop meaningful strategies to help students harness the possibilities of intersectionality. This chapter explores ways to help students with disabilities develop the skills necessary to negotiate their multiple identities through experiential learning and by maximizing collaboration among campus units.

Experiential Learning

Experiential learning requires students to grapple with their multiple identities to execute shared learning through discursive acts (Gubrium & Holstein, 2001). By engaging students in experiential learning as they enter academe, we can hasten the process by which they form their own identities. Experiential learning in introductory courses (a) helps students identify, test, and reflect upon their values in relation to other students, the academy, and the local community; (b) teaches students responsible research practices and how to situate knowledge in various contexts; (c) teaches them to use writing to think critically and solve problems; and (d) creates a safe space for students to develop soft skills that will inspire confidence, build character, and enrich the rest of their lives.

Consider Chuck, a low-vision student who parlayed his hobby— inventing sports equipment for visually challenged people—into national recognition in a competition for entrepreneurs. Chuck's story began in Purdue University Calumet's First-Year Writing Program in his first semester at our university. He is a perfect example of a freshman student with multiple identities who thrived in our program largely owing to the use of universal design and an experiential learning pedagogy. Chuck had a dream of building his fledgling nonprofit—a sports-centered association for the blind—into a strong and competitive global organization. Someday. He had no idea that an assignment in a general education course could catapult his dream.

Over the course of the semester, Chuck and his instructor developed a collaborative relationship in which they discussed multimodal methods to aid in his learning. All the course assignments and writing prompts were distributed in various formats (Wilson and Lewiecki-Wilson, 2008). For example, Chuck could increase the print size of documents and use the PDF read-aloud function. Most significantly, however, the instructor learned about Chuck's dream of entrepreneurship and allowed him to focus his research and writing for the semester on exploring his passion. Because of the collaborative learning situation between the student and the instructor, and the flexibility in assignments and prompts, Chuck acquired the knowledge and confidence to take what he had written in the classroom and enter a nationwide contest for entrepreneurs. He finished in the top 10.

A Collective Approach to Multiple Identities

Students like Chuck are not only learning transferable skills, they are learning the language of self-advocacy. If the typical freshman is uncertain about experiential learning projects, which partner students with off-campus community organizations, imagine the feelings of a freshman with a disability who is away from his or her parents and support system for the first time. The reward is, however, that students with a disability emerge from these experiences with new identities created from a narrative of enhanced self-worth. Faculty and staff have a responsibility to help students cultivate this sense of self-worth early on in their education, so they have the fortitude to seek the resources and support they need. Henry, Fuerth, and Figliozzi (2010), in their article "Gay with a Disability: A College Student's Multiple Cultural Journey," discussed the roadblocks that surface for students with multiple identities in the university setting. Their assessment revealed that students were unable to find support in just one department; rather, they were required to segment their identities and bounce among departments for services, which meant prioritizing one aspect of their identity over another. One student said that although the disability services office provided adaptive resources, he felt uncomfortable with the staff and "perceived the counselors to be impersonal and unapproachable toward issues outside of his disabilities" (Henry et al., 2010, p. 383). The same student sought support for his sexual orientation at the university's counseling center. The center permitted a minimal number of sessions at no charge, but the support ended when the fees kicked in and the student was unable to pay for private counseling.

Both academic and nonacademic units should formalize outreach strategies to maximize delivery systems that meet students' physical, psychological, and social needs. In our writing program at Purdue University Calumet, we have deepened our relationship with the disability services office to broaden the conversation and training where universal design concepts are concerned. Embracing the lesbian, gay, bisexual, transgender, queer/questioning, and ally community has meant mining our own instructional staff to encourage a volunteer to provide SafeZone training for our staff. As defined by the Gay Alliance (2012), the "SafeZone program was created to develop, enhance and maintain environments in workplaces, schools and other social settings that are culturally competent and supportive to LGBT individuals, as well as straight identified people who care about diversity, equality and inclusion" (para. 3).

Student affairs professionals can help students explore the possibilities of their multiple identities by adopting the following best practices:

- **F**ind units (academic and nonacademic) that might be beneficial partners and maximize those relationships to create clear pathways for students to seek assistance.
- **E**stablish formal channels for sharing the university agenda, legislative updates, and disability best practices. Improved communication results in programming that addresses the whole rather than fragments of student identities.
- **E**mbrace opportunities for experiential learning with students who have disabilities. This kind of learning is an inclusive and safe way to help students learn to self-advocate and develop transferable skills, while managing the added dimension of intersectionality.
- **L**isten to students—in your office, in class, in the cafeteria, at the bus stop. Too often our work carries us far afield from what should be our number one priority: students.

At the end of the day, changing the landscape of working with students with disabilities must be a collective enterprise that engages not only students but every echelon of the institution and every aspect of society. Collaboration is the key to taking a stand for one and making a difference for all.

References

Collins, P. H. (2005). *Black sexual politics: African Americans, gender, and the new racism.* New York, NY: Routledge.

Gay Alliance. (2012). *SafeZone training programs.* Retrieved from http://www.gayalliance.org/safezonet.html

Gubrium, J. F., & Holstein, J. A. (2001). *Institutional selves: Troubled identities in a postmodern world.* Thousand Oaks, CA: Sage.

Henry, W. J., Fuerth, K., & Figliozzi, J. (2010). Gay with a disability: A college student's multiple cultural journey. *College Student Journal, 44*(2), 377–388.

Sims, C. D. L. (2013). *Disrupting race, claiming colonization: Collective remembering and rhetorical colonization in negotiating (Native) American identities in the U.S.* (Doctoral dissertation). Available from ProQuest Dissertations and Theses database. (UMI No. 3562050)

Wilson, J. C., & Lewiecki-Wilson, C. (2008). Constructing a third space: Disability studies, the teaching of English, and institutional transformation. In C. Lewiecki-Wilson & B. J. Brueggemann (Eds.), *Disability and the teaching of writing: A critical sourcebook* (pp. 153–157) Boston: Bedford/ St. Martin's.

Chapter 20

Challenging the Status Quo

Dhanfu E. Elston

Leaders must have the courage to shift institutional culture, marshal the political capital required to align practice with philosophy, and challenge the status quo. As a senior administrator who aspires to be a vice president and a professional whose roles have varied between student and academic affairs, one of my overarching goals has been to pursue the highest level of access as we seek to promote student success in an inclusive learning environment. The foundations of my inclusive values are in my experiences as a Black male undergraduate student; these values were further cultivated through my graduate school training in the areas of educational policy and college student development. As upcoming educators and administrators, we were encouraged to be mindful of our campus environments.

A New Perspective on Disability

My first interaction with a staff member with a disability occurred during the interview process, when I suddenly realized that she had limited mobility. Few of my counterparts had had any experience with colleagues who had a disability, and I had not been apprised of any accommodation request from this candidate. I had felt the discomfort of some of the White interviewers during my own hiring process—this experience created a subtle cultural connection between the two of us. After I hired her, I continued to learn about her lived experiences and how our campus could benefit from her personal and professional background with disabilities, universal design, and inclusivity.

For years, I had worked with administrators to ensure that we were compliant with the Americans with Disabilities Act of 1990 (ADA), but the policies were often viewed merely as items to check off the list. No policy brief, white paper, or conference presentation influenced me more than a walk across campus with a colleague who uses a scooter. I found that many of our ramps and entrances were inconveniently located and not user-friendly.

One of the greatest contributions of our new staff member is the diversity of thought she has contributed to our campus presentations and curricular offerings. Faculty and staff are revisiting processes to provide a more inclusive environment, which can serve as a retention tool for under-served and at-risk student populations. A universally designed educational environment not only provides comprehensive access but also forces us to reconcile the fact that our "model of learning is out of date and inaccurate" (Fried, 2006, p. 3).

Scholars continue to promote the benefits of a diverse environment for student learning and development. Sue (2003) argued that monocultural learning environments, curricula, and pedagogy are a disservice to students. Therefore, educators and administrators must also realize that just being in an environment with disabled students does not automatically lead to credibility from the disabled student population. What must happen is the process of building cultural competencies stemming from

192

a mutual learning process, leading to understanding, accountability, and results. So the question becomes, how do we as administrators systemically enforce a culture that is supportive not only of students, but also of colleagues and administrators, with disabilities?

The focus on student retention continues to dominate the agenda of policymakers, but the connection between disability and retention is hard to clarify, as many students may never self-identify as disabled, especially if they have "hidden" disabilities. People who are living the disability experience can be found throughout our ranks. The diversity they bring could be informing our practice in significant ways if we provided an inclusive and welcoming environment that respects disability as part of the framework.

Becoming an Ally

Higher education institutions often express a desire for a diverse student body. However, being an ally of people with disabilities on campus can be difficult, especially at a college or university with a deeply entrenched history of exclusion. In his novel *1984*, George Orwell (1949) introduced the concept of "doublethink"—simultaneously believing in two contradictory ideals. Although they may agree on the need for campus improvement and advocacy, some administrators and faculty members do not want to hear a critique of the institution and, more important, lack the political will to allocate appropriate resources to ameliorate the issues.

Structural diversity is about numbers, and numbers are not enough to create a truly inclusive campus. Listening to and learning from my colleague with a disability and reflecting on my own personal identities have enabled me to become a stronger advocate and ally. How can we claim to be the future leaders in higher education if we fail to reconcile our own issues and lack of understanding when our comfort zones are affected?

Ultimately, higher education administrators must stop wasting time and act. Often, we spend more time oppressing than empowering students with disabilities, who face the daunting task of dealing with power and privilege. Thinking about the commonalities and intersections of identities in my own life helped me define key areas of support that I would want for myself and that I need to provide as an ally for students and colleagues with disabilities. I suggest the following:

- Recruit students and colleagues with disabilities to join you at the policymaking table. Use them as experts and invaluable resources.
- Listen to their stories and use the data they provide to challenge long-held institutional beliefs and practices that run contrary to the goal of inclusion.
- Support members of campus communities who have disabilities, even if you experience hostility from senior-level administrators.

Marginalization of students and staff with disabilities is not just a social condition but a scholarly condition as well. Integrated learning does not happen only in the classroom but also in the shared experiences of all campus stakeholders. As I continue on my professional path, I want to be part of a new wave of higher education leaders who are committed to being at the forefront of access issues. If we are to fully leverage the talent and expertise in our ranks and improve the retention and success of our students, faculty, and staff with disabilities, we have no choice but to step up to the plate and work actively as agents of change in our institutions.

References

Americans with Disabilities Act of 1990, 42 U.S.C., § 12101 *et seq.* (2011).

Fried, J. (2006). Rethinking learning. In R. Keeling (Ed.), *Learning reconsidered 2: Implementing a campus-wide focus on the student experience* (pp. 3–9). Washington, DC: American College Personnel Association, Association of College and University Housing Officers-International, Association of College Unions-International, National Academic Advising Association, National Association for Campus Activities, National Association of Student Personnel Administrators, National Intramural-Recreational Sports Association.

Orwell, G. (1949). *Nineteen eighty-four*. London, England: Secker and Warburg.

Sue, D. W. (2003). *Overcoming our racism: The journey to liberation*. San Francisco, CA: Jossey-Bass.

The Authors

Jean Ashmore is disability director emeritus and retired lecturer from Rice University. She served on the Board of Directors for the Association on Higher Education and Disability (AHEAD) from 2003 to 2012, culminating as president from 2010 to 2012. As a past-president, Ashmore represents AHEAD with a number of organizations. During her tenure on the AHEAD board, Ashmore oversaw expansion of the regional affiliate program, substantially increased international engagement, and implemented new operational structures for enhanced association effectiveness. Additionally, she coordinated revisions to disability service standards with the Council for the Advancement of Standards in Higher Education that reflect professional practice changes incorporating cultural/social rather than medical perspectives on disability. Ashmore is a regular conference presenter and instructor on disability in higher education at national and regional meetings of AHEAD. Prior to establishing the Disability Department at Rice University, Ashmore's professional experience included school counseling, as well as vocational and rehabilitation counseling for the Veterans Administration and other organizations. In addition to consulting on disability topics, Ashmore sits on the Think College Wisconsin steering committee and assists Special Olympics Wisconsin. Ashmore holds a Bachelor of Arts degree from the University of California, Los Angeles, and a Master of Science degree from California State University, Los Angeles.

Bea Awoniyi, PhD, is the assistant vice president for student affairs at Santa Fe College and the college's ombudsman. She oversees all of the grant programs within the Division of Student Affairs and participates in the collegewide grant process and the college's efforts to internationalize the campus. Awoniyi served as a disability services professional from 1990 to 2012, developing programs, writing standards for services, and participating in statewide and interagency collaborations for effective transition, inclusion, and engagement of students with disabilities in Colorado, Iowa, and Florida. She currently serves as president-elect of the Association on Higher Education and Disability (AHEAD). She is also a founding member and past president of the AHEAD state affiliate Florida AHEAD. She has served as the NASPA Region III representative for the Disability Knowledge Community, and is a member of the International Ombudsman Association. Originally from Nigeria, Awoniyi received her Bachelor of Science, magna cum laude, and Master of Science degrees from Southern Illinois University Carbondale and her PhD from Colorado State University in Fort Collins, Colorado. She was the 2011 recipient of the Ronald E. Blosser Dedicated Service Award, AHEAD's highest honor, and was the first recipient of the Fredrick A. Fay Pioneer Award from Florida State University.

Jamie Axelrod earned a BA in psychology from New York University and an MS in counseling at the University of Wisconsin–Madison. After graduating with his master's degree, Axelrod began working as a mental health therapist in Valparaiso, Indiana, and Lander, Wyoming. After 13 years at community mental health centers, he went to work for Protection and Advocacy Systems, Inc., a disability rights advocacy law firm, where he served as an advocate assisting individuals with disabilities with claims that their civil rights had been violated. Axelrod joined the Disability Resources team at Northern Arizona University in August 2007 as a program coordinator and became the director of the Disability Resources program in October 2009.

Karen Bishop Morris, PhD, is the director of the First-Year Writing Program and director of the Writing Center at Purdue University Calumet. She is responsible for curriculum development, program assessment, faculty evaluation, mentoring, and professional development for the writing program. She also trains graduate students in the theory and practice of writing pedagogy. She served as director of the writing program at the University of Southern Indiana, and has been recognized for her work with faculty across the disciplines to form public writing partnerships and to integrate writing into their content areas. In 2011, she received an Experiential Learning Course Design and Development Award to assess the integration of experiential learning across multiple sections of writing courses. Her scholarship focuses on using the teaching of writing to help students see their academic preparation as transferable to the workplace, and mediating literacy issues for first-generation and nontraditional students. She has been a frequent speaker and workshop presenter at the annual meeting for the Conference on College Composition and Communication, National Council of Teachers of English and Computers and Writing. Her work has appeared in *English Education, WPA: The Journal for Writing Program Administrators,* and several edited collections.

Sheryl Burgstahler, PhD, is the director of the Disabilities, Opportunities, Internetworking, and Technology Center, the director of accessible technology services, and an affiliate professor in the College of Education at the University of Washington. She has published articles and delivered presentations at national and international conferences that focus on universal design of distance learning, websites and multimedia, computer labs, instruction, student services, and other applications in education; and the management of electronic communities, work-based learning activities, and transition programs for youth with disabilities. She is the author or co-author of eight books on using the Internet with pre-college students and directing e-mentoring and transition programs, and is the lead author and editor of the book *Universal Design in Higher Education: From Principles* *to Practice* (Harvard Education Press, 2008). Burgstahler and her projects have received many awards, including the AHEAD Professional Recognition Award, the National Information Infrastructure Award in Education, the President's Award for Mentoring, the Golden Apple Award in Education, the AHEAD Program Recognition Award, and the Harry J. Murphy Catalyst Award.

Jacquelyn Bustos is a graduate teaching assistant at Purdue University Calumet where she is pursuing an MA in English, specializing in rhetoric and composition. She is also the assistant to the director of the First-Year Writing Program. Bustos has experience educating and inspiring students with various learning differences, such as dyslexia, autism spectrum disorders, and various physical and psychological disabilities (including attention deficit hyperactivity disorder, bipolar disorder, and schizophrenia).

Diane Ciarletta has been a career counselor for 25 years at Northeastern University where she currently serves as interim director of career development. She is passionate about working with students with disabilities, and together with colleagues from the Northeastern University Disability Resource Center and Co-op Department, formed NuConnect, an innovative model for assisting disabled students with finding employment. Ciarletta is also passionate about helping students learn about nonprofit careers and finding work that makes a difference. She created nuC.A.U.S.E. Careers (Creating Awareness and Understanding of Social Engagement Careers), a Northeastern University Career Services initiative designed to connect students to socially minded employers and teach students about careers in the nonprofit sector. She also enjoys using the Myers-Briggs Type Indicator (MBTI) for career development and team building. She has worked with groups on- and off-campus to use the MBTI as a way to help teams improve their effectiveness.

Eileen Connell Berger is the assistant director of the Office of Student Affairs and Access and disability services administrator at the Harvard Graduate School of Education (HGSE). She is committed to the complex issues of inclusion, equal access, equal opportunity, and social justice with emphasis on students with disabilities. Berger worked as a speech and hearing specialist, educator, administrator, and grant writer in K–12 public and private schools for 15 years, developing policy, programs, curriculum, and training for parents, children, and mainstream educators. She has worked in higher education for 18 years as a director of disability services. She has created services and programs for students with disabilities at Bunker Hill Community College in Charlestown, Massachusetts; Salem State University in Salem, Massachusetts; and HGSE. She holds an MSEd and an EdD (ABD); has New York State, New York City, and Massachusetts teacher certification; and is certified in assistive technology. Berger is currently co-chair of the NASPA Disability Knowledge Community. She presents with colleagues and students at conferences yearly, and is an advisory board member for the Heroism and Disability Initiative in the Heroic Imagination Project of Philip Zimbardo at Stanford University and the NASPA Commission on Equity and Inclusion. She is currently writing about accommodations for advanced graduate students with disabilities and is chair of the Brookline Commission on Disabilities, for the Town of Brookline, Massachusetts.

Edwin A. Coolbaugh, II, is currently the assistant dean/director of residence life at the College of the Holy Cross in Worcester, Massachusetts. He has served as an assistant dean of students at the College of Saint Elizabeth in Morristown, New Jersey, and area coordinator/hall director at Eastern Connecticut State University. He received his bachelor's and master's degrees from Keene State College in Keene, New Hampshire.

Jennifer L. DelRey, PhD, earned combined doctoral degrees in counseling psychology and school psychology from Florida State University. She currently serves as the disability services coordinator at the College of the Holy Cross in Worcester, Massachusetts, and also has a private consulting practice in central Massachusetts. DelRey's areas of specialization include students (early childhood, K–12, and college) with special needs, with particular interests in attention deficit hyperactivity disorder, learning disabilities, social-emotional disabilities, psycho-educational evaluation, and psychological trauma. DelRey enjoys consulting to school districts, colleges, parents, and attorneys and providing training and educational outreach, in addition to advocating for students requiring alternative school placements. She has also served as an expert in juvenile and family court matters, and serves as a guardian *ad Litem* for children and families through the Massachusetts probate and family courts. DelRey is a member of the Advisory Board of the Child Trauma Training Center at the University of Massachusetts Medical School, and also serves as the NASPA Region I corepresentative for the Disability Knowledge Community.

Gaeir Dietrich is the director of the High Tech Center Training Unit of the California Community Colleges located at De Anza College in Cupertino, California. She is a nationally recognized expert in the area of alternate media and is a founding member of the Association on Higher Education and Disability (AHEAD) E-text Solutions Group and codeveloper of the AHEAD E-text Institute. Dietrich serves on several advisory boards, including Bookshare, the Alternate Text Production Center, AHEAD, and the Silicon Valley Independent Living Center. She led the Veterans Resource Center project for the California Community Colleges Chancellor's Office. In 2010–2011, she served as the chair for the national advisory commission on Accessible Instructional Materials in Postsecondary Education.

Dhanfu E. Elston, PhD, is the director of student success and transition for Purdue University Calumet. He has more than 18 years of progressive management experience in higher education policy, college student development, retention, and academic curriculum at a broad range of institutions (public and private schools, historically Black colleges and universities [HBCUs], 4-year institutions, and community colleges). His professional tenure has also included student and academic affairs positions at Clark Atlanta University and Georgia State University. Elston received bachelor's and master's degrees from Clark Atlanta University, and a doctorate in educational policy studies from Georgia State University. His commitment to the intercultural growth of students has led to his appointment as a lead facilitator for LeaderShape, a 6-day curricular leadership institute designed to encourage students to "lead with integrity," where he facilitates national sessions at premier colleges and universities throughout the United States. He is a member of the NASPA African American Knowledge Community Leadership Team, chairperson of the NASPA HBCU Council, and former recipient of the NASPA Region III Research and Assessment Grant.

Scott N. Friedman is the director of disability services and 504/ADA coordinator with the Center for Access and Disability Services at William Rainey Harper College in Palatine, Illinois. He started as an adjunct professor teaching students with intellectual disabilities at Elmhurst College in Elmhurst, Illinois, and also previously held a disability services position at the University of Illinois at Chicago. The department under his current leadership works to positively influence practice through use of the Social Model, and annually provides access services and accommodations to more than 1,300 students with disabilities. Friedman holds master's degrees in both adult and higher education and special education, and is completing his PhD research in disability studies at the University of Illinois at Chicago. His scholarly interests include disability-based professional development, documentation practices, and innovative academic programs that support students with disabilities. He serves as the NASPA Region IV-East representative for the Disability Knowledge Community, and as cochair to the Documentation Subcommittee for the Illinois Board of Higher Education's Disabilities Advisory Committee.

Christie Gilson, PhD, is a disability rights advocate and has provided reasonable accommodations to students with disabilities at three universities. She has also taught courses in education, disability studies, and writing at three postsecondary institutions. President Obama has appointed Gilson to the J. William Fulbright Foreign Scholarship Board. The board is charged with reviewing applications for Fulbright and affiliated grants to

foreign and domestic students and scholars. Gilson's research interests include transition from secondary to postsecondary education for students
with disabilities. She has authored or coauthored 10 peer-reviewed articles
and a chapter for a book about inclusive education in the Asia-Pacific region published by Routledge.

Paul D. Grossman, JD, recently retired after 40 years of service at the U.S.
Department of Education, Office for Civil Rights (OCR), 30 years as its
chief regional attorney in San Francisco, California, and 20 years leading
its national disability law and policy training program. Grossman also
serves as an advisor to both OCR and the U.S. Department of Justice on
disability in higher education law and policy, including higher education
programs and services for wounded warriors. Grossman is now in his 12th
year as an adjunct professor of disability law at the University of California
Hastings College of the Law. He is coauthor of *The Law of Disability Discrimination* (8th Ed.) (Lexis-Nexis, 2013). He is a frequent keynote speaker
and is on the conference faculties of the Association on Higher Education
and Disability, the National Association of ADA Coordinators, and the
Texas Higher Education Law Conference.

Robyn L. Hudson is an assistant director in Services for Students with
Disabilities at the Virginia Polytechnic Institute and State University
(Virginia Tech). She earned her PhD in curriculum and instruction from
Virginia Tech in 2013, her MSW from Radford University in 1999, and is
a licensed clinical social worker in the Commonwealth of Virginia. Prior
to assuming the position at Virginia Tech in January 2005, she was the
assistant director of the Disability Resource Office at Radford University.
She has been an adjunct faculty at New River Community College, a child
and family therapist, juvenile probation officer, and medical social worker.

Steven M. Janosik, PhD, is the chair of the Department of Educational
Leadership and Policy Studies at Virginia Polytechnic Institute and State
University (Virginia Tech) and also serves as associate professor and coor-

dinator for the Higher Education program. Janosik has more than 20 years of experience in college administration. He has authored or coauthored more than 85 refereed journal articles, book chapters, and policy reports on the topics of campus crime, college administration, higher education law and policy, liability and risk management, professional standards, and ethics. Janosik is a frequent presenter at national conferences on these topics and is the cofounder of the National Assessment of Student Conduct Adjudications Processes Project.

Devva Kasnitz, PhD, has worked in disability studies for more than 35 years. She recently concluded work with the Association on Higher Education and Disability and is an adjunct professor at The City University of New York. She was on founding boards of the Society for Disability Studies, the Anthropology and Disability Research Interest Group, and the Association of Programs for Rural Independent Living, and she has mentored a generation of disability studies scholars in the United States, Australia, and Guatemala. Trained as a cultural geographer (Clark University) and anthropologist (University of Michigan), she did postdoctoral work in policy and medicine at Northwestern University and the University of California, San Francisco.

Neal E. Lipsitz, PhD, is the associate dean for student development at the College of the Holy Cross in Worcester, Massachusetts. As an associate dean, Lipsitz oversees the counseling center, health services, wellness programming, and disability services. A licensed psychologist in the Commonwealth of Massachusetts, he has specialized in college mental health. After earning his PhD in counseling psychology, Lipsitz was director of the Counseling Center at Holy Cross prior to becoming an associate dean. He had also worked as a staff psychologist at several college counseling centers and has taught a number of psychology and counseling courses at Holy Cross and at Boston College. He also maintains a private practice in Newton Centre, Massachusetts, where he sees adolescents and adults.

Rachel Luna is currently the assistant director for the Center for Community Involvement at the University of the Pacific in Stockton, California. She earned her MA in college student personnel at Bowling Green State University in Bowling Green, Ohio, and her BA in mass communications and education at the University of California, Berkeley. Luna has held various roles in the American College Personnel Association (ACPA), including member of the Equity and Inclusion Advisory Committee and social media coordinator of the Multiracial Network. She was also awarded the Disability Ally Fellowship Award from ACPA's Standing Committee on Disability.

John D. Mikelson (SFC retired) is a disabled veteran from the United States Army (1978–2004). He graduated from the University of Iowa (UI) with a bachelor's degree in history and a master's degree in higher education in December 2008. Mikelson helped form the University of Iowa Veterans Association and established a Veterans Transition Center, where he currently works as the center's coordinator. He serves on the UI Council for Disability Awareness, the Iowa Vocational Rehabilitation Services Council, and is the veterans affairs advisor for the Association of Non-Traditional Students in Higher Education. He previously served on the boards of the National Alliance on Mental Illness of Johnson County and the National Academic Advising Association Advising Veterans, Military Students and Family Members Interest Group, and is a cofounder of the Student Veterans of America. He is currently chair of the NASPA Veterans Knowledge Community and president of the Johnson County Military Affairs Association.

Kaela Parks is the director of disability services at Portland Community College and president of the Oregon Association for Higher Education and Disability. She is past director of disability support services at the University of Alaska Anchorage, where she led a collaborative Web accessibility initiative in partnership with the state and designed and taught courses on disability in the media, assistive technology, universal design, college survival skills, and multimedia accessibility. She has worked on federal grants related to universal design and presents frequently at regional and national conferences. She is cochair of the Association for Higher Education and Disability Standing Committee on Technology and past-chair of the NASPA Disability Knowledge Community. Her writing has focused on transition, social justice, and information technology accessibility.

Veronica L. Porter, PhD, is an associate professor and coordinator of cooperative education at Northeastern University in Boston, Massachusetts, and has served as the cooperative education liaison to the Disability Resource Center for more than 20 years. She develops partnerships with employers to provide experiential opportunities for students and teaches the curriculum of the Cooperative Education Program. Her research areas include outcomes of student learning relative to cooperative and experiential education, as well as employment of college students and graduates with disabilities. She has conducted presentations internationally, nationally, and regionally. She received the Dr. Robert Greenberg Award for Innovation, established by Career Opportunities for Students with Disabilities; the Practice Oriented Education Special Recognition Award at Northeastern University; and the Disability Resource Center Extraordinary Contribution Award. She is a member of the Phi Beta Delta Honor Society for International Scholars and Students. Her doctor of philosophy degree is in law, policy, and society.

Cerise Roth-Vinson is the chief operating officer at Mobility International USA. She manages the National Clearinghouse on Disability and Exchange, sponsored by the U.S. Department of State, to increase the participation of people with disabilities in the broad range of international exchange programs. Since 1997, Roth-Vinson has worked in the field of international exchange and disability rights and is an expert on disability inclusion. She studied language and conducted research in Yemen, participated on international volunteer work camps in Turkey and Japan, studied abroad in France, and volunteered with the Peace Corps in the Republic of Gambia. She holds an MA in international development from the University of Oregon and a BA in political science from Southwestern University in Georgetown, Texas.

Michele Scheib specializes in advising students with disabilities traveling to and from the United States, and providing technical assistance to colleges and universities and organizations on disability inclusion and international exchange. Scheib is project specialist of the National Clearinghouse on Disability and Exchange, which is sponsored by the U.S. Department of State and administered by Mobility International USA. Since 1998, she has been initiating projects involving the Internet, outreach, social media, research, publications, events, and presentations. Scheib has a BA in cultural anthropology from Pennsylvania State University and an MA in comparative and international development education from the University of Minnesota, where she addressed the topic of students with non-apparent disabilities in education abroad. She also assisted with the U.S. Department of Education-funded Access Abroad project for enhancing study abroad for students with disabilities. Scheib visited with disability organizations in Northeast Thailand on a Rotary scholarship and has also studied abroad with the School for International Training in Kenya, after which she volunteered as a teacher for deaf children in rural Kenya.

Marci Shaffer is an Asperger syndrome specialist in the Disability Resource Center at Northeastern University (NU) in Boston, Massachusetts. She is a cofounder of NuConnect, a strategic working partnership among the Disability Resource Center, Co-Op Program, and Career Services. She also manages a thriving private career coaching practice for college students and adults with Asperger syndrome and related disorders. Before stepping into the higher education setting, Shaffer held key positions in corporate human resources, including talent acquisition and training roles.

Matthew Springer is the director of disability services at Indiana University Southeast, serving in that position since 2008. Matt received his undergraduate degree in English at the University of Kentucky, where he was awarded the Adelstein Award for Service by the institution's Office of Disability Services. He received his master's degree in educational leadership from Wright State University in Dayton, Ohio, where he also coordinated athletic and recreational programs for students with disabilities. He has been active in his field's national organization, the Association on Higher Education and Disability (AHEAD), for almost a decade. He is also the chair for AHEAD's special interest group on student athletes with disabilities.

Jane Thierfeld Brown, EdD, is the director of student services at the University of Connecticut School of Law, and director of College Autism Spectrum and assistant clinical professor at the Yale School of Medicine Child Study Center. She has worked in disability services for more than 34 years. Brown received her BA in speech pathology, MS in counseling, and MA in education from the University of Rhode Island. She holds an EdD from Columbia University, Teachers College. Her main research interests are students with autism/Asperger's in higher education and students with disabilities in high-stakes graduate programs. She consults at many higher education institutions and is a frequent speaker at conferences. She is a coauthor of *Students with Asperger Syndrome: A Guide for College Personnel* (Autism Asperger Publishing Company [AAPC], 2009), *The Parent's Guide to College for Students on the Autism Spectrum* (AAPC, 2012), and *Social Behavior and Self Management* (AAPC, 2012). Brown consults with colleges, students, and families across the United States on issues for students with autism spectrum disorders.

Tom L. Thompson is the former director of disability services and the ADA coordinator at Harper College (1980–2010). During that time, the department grew from serving 100 students to serving more than 1,200. In addition, several innovative, educational support programs were created, including ones that focused on students who are deaf/hard of hearing, students with learning disabilities, and students with Asperger syndrome. He has written and managed grants totaling more than $6,750,000. He holds an MA in rehabilitation counseling and a BA in psychology and philosophy. He has served twice on the Board of the Association on Higher Education and Disability (AHEAD), was a founding member of the Illinois-Iowa AHEAD chapter, and has presented at numerous conferences on program development, budgeting, and program assessment. He has had leadership roles as the former chair of the Disabilities Advisory Committee of the Illinois Board of Higher Education and is the chair of a national AHEAD task force on students with intellectual disabilities in postsecondary education.

Mary Lee Vance, PhD, has directed disability services at the 2-year and 4-year campuses of George Mason University, the University of Wisconsin–Superior, and the University of Montana. She is past cochair of the NASPA Disability Knowledge Community. She edited *Advising Students with Disabilities: Striving for Universal Success* (2ⁿᵈ Ed.) (National Academic Advising Association [NACADA], 2009), as well as the anthology *DISABLED Faculty and Staff in a Disabling Society: Multiple Identities in Higher Education* (Association on Higher Education and Disability [AHEAD], 2007). She served six consecutive years as a member of the AHEAD Board of Directors and as a practice brief reviewer for the *Journal of Postsecondary Education and Disability (JPED)*. In addition, she has published more than 23 chapters and articles in textbooks, refereed journals, and periodicals on a wide range of topics, including accommodating wounded warriors and universal design in the curriculum. In 2013, she co-authored the revisions to the disability services standards for the Council for the Advancement of Standards in Higher Education. Currently, she serves on the editorial board for *JPED*, reviews for the *NACADA Journal*, and consults on a variety of higher education topics.

Lorraine E. Wolf, PhD, is the director of disability services at Boston University. She holds a doctorate in clinical neuropsychology from the City University of New York and has more than 25 years of experience working with children, adolescents, and adults with neurodevelopmental disorders. She has taught experimental psychology, assessment, and neuropsychology at the undergraduate and graduate levels. Wolf has published and presented nationally and internationally on issues for students with attention and learning disorders, psychiatric disabilities, and autism spectrum disorders. She holds faculty appointments in psychiatry and in rehabilitation sciences at Boston University. She was a coeditor of *Adult Attention Deficit Disorders: Brain Mechanisms and Life Outcomes* (New York Academy of Sciences, 2001), the senior coeditor of *Learning Disorders in Adults: Contemporary Issues* (Psychology Press, 2008), and a coauthor of *Students with Asperger Syndrome: A Guide for College Personnel* (Autism Asperger Publishing Company [AAPC], 2009) and *The Parent's Guide to College for Students on the Autism Spectrum* (AAPC, 2012). Along with Jane Thierfeld Brown, she developed a model of service delivery for college students titled "Strategic Education for students with Autism Spectrum Disorders." Wolf's interests include the neuropsychology of attention disorders, and developing effective services for students with autism spectrum and other psychiatric disabilities in higher education.

Index

Index

Thomas, C., 27

Thompson, Tom L., 97

Thornton, M., 32

Threat assessment, 137, 182

Ticketing, 15, 17

"Time, manner, and duration" necessary to perform major life activity, 10

Toth v. Slippery Rock University of Pennsylvania (2010), 180

Toyota Motor Manufacturing, Kentucky, Inc. v. Williams (2002), 4

Training
    department staffs on disability laws, 137–138
    disability services staff on disability laws, 71
    to respond appropriately to students with disabilities, 182
    on veterans with disabilities, 94–95

Transition and Postsecondary Programs for Students with Intellectual Disabilities (TPSIDs) grants, 99–100, 104, 105–106

Transition programs, need for, 120, 136, 145–150
    comprehensive transition programs (CTPs), 106
    from IDEA to ADA, 146–147
    models of bridge programs, 148–149
    multidisciplinary collaboration, 149
    self-advocacy of students with disabilities as part of, 147–148

Transitory and minor impairments, 8

Traumatic brain injury (TBI), 85

Tutoring, 136

Twitter, 55, 61

U

Unemployment rate of people with disabilities, 151

United Kingdom's social model of disability, 27

United Nations Convention on the Rights of Persons with Disabilities (CRPD), 25

United States
    history of disability in U.S., 22–24
    theoretical models used in, 27

Universal design (UD), 25, 35–48
    advisory board or task force, 43
    background, 35–36
    benefits of, 42, 44, 81, 192
    challenges of, 37–43
    checklist, 42–43

construction projects, 142–143

on continuum, 38

defined, 171

events accessible to all, 43

Florida Consortium on Postsecondary Education and Intellectual Disabilities using, 106

implications for practice, 43, 57, 61–62

information technology, 25, 42–43, 80–81

of instruction, 28, 38–42

for intellectual disabilities, 107

for international students with disabilities, 176

online Universal Design in Higher Education group, 43

physical environments and products, 42, 142–143

planning, policies, and evaluation, 42, 43

professional development, 43, 81

researchers and practitioners identifying strategies for, 39–41

staff, 42, 43

in student affairs technology, 61–62

student retention and, 36–37

of student services, 42–43

student veterans and, 91

of study abroad programs, 166–167

in technology and online environments, 141–144

Universal Design in Higher Education, From Principles to Practice (Burgstahler & Cory), 108

University of Alaska Anchorage, 130

University of California, Berkeley (UCB), 79–80

University of California Education Abroad Program (UCEAP), 168

University of Illinois at Urbana-Champaign's residence halls, 161

University of Massachusetts Boston
    Coordinating Center at Institute for Community Inclusion, 99–100
    Think College Coordinating Center, 105

University of Massachusetts' Dartmouth study (2011), 54

University of Minnesota's PASS IT (Pedagogy and Student Services for Institutional Transformation) project, 57

University of North Florida, partnering with Florida Consortium on Postsecondary

221